"Cynthia is the consummate energy and passion for helping other small businesses is evident to all who know her and this book is her way of sharing the knowledge so that others can thrive and grow. I highly recommend it."

—Rob Fowler, president and CEO, Small Business Association of Michigan

"Cynthia Kay has small business success in her DNA. Her instincts about business development, people development, financial management and organizational growth are spot on. Small Business for Big Thinkers gives us a chance to learn from Cynthia's experiences and get a head start on the growing economic boom that is small business. "

—Beth Kelly, managing partner, HR Collaborative and author of *The EE Gap*

"Cynthia has always been positive and confident in her business pursuits and with this book you now get to find out how and why she has been so successful. This book is full of the nitty gritty advice all small business owners need to make it in today's volatile world!"

—Fred Keller, chair and CEO, Cascade Engineering, Past Chair Department of Commerce Manufacturing Advisory Council,

"Cynthia Kay, along with the outstanding business owners she profiles, provides the kind of fresh thinking that business owners need. Her unconventional strategies for attracting big business can benefit companies, no matter how large or small. It's a great read!"

—Jim Dunlap, senior executive vice president, regional and commercial banking director, Huntington Bank

"Cynthia Kay has presented a number of training sessions for BDO. Her insights on how to respond to RFPs and create great presentations to connect and deepen the relationship with large customers can benefit businesses large and small."

—Matthew K. Becker, regional managing partner, tax services, BDO USA, LLP

SMALL BUSINESS
FOR
BIG THINKERS

UNCONVENTIONAL STRATEGIES TO CONNECT

WITH AND WIN BIG BUSINESS

CYNTHIA KAY

Pompton Plains, NJ

SMALL BUSINESS FOR BIG THINKERS
EDITED BY ROGER SHEETY
Cover design by Rob Johnson/Toprotype
Printed in the U.S.A.

To order this title, please call toll-free 1-800-CAREER-1 (NJ and Canada: 201-848-0310) to order using VISA or MasterCard, or for further information on books from Career Press.

The Career Press, Inc.
220 West Parkway, Unit 12
Pompton Plains, NJ 07444
www.careerpress.com

Library of Congress Cataloging-in-Publication Data
CIP Data Available Upon Request.

To my parents, Ann and Gus, who taught me to be a big thinker, not only in business but in life.

ACKNOWLEDGMENTS

It is a simple fact. I would not have had the time to take on the task of writing this book, if it were not for my sister, Vicki, and her husband, Charles. In addition to running an impressive small business, they are also caring for our parents day to day. They are my heroes. The support of my brother, Steve, and sister-in-law, Bess, along with family and friends has been immeasurable. My thanks go out to the staff at Cynthia Kay and Company. These are individuals who share my love of small business, and they prove it every day.

My journey to become an author began a few years ago, but changed the day I met John Willig. The event was a "Meet the Agents Day" in Philadelphia, a kind of speed dating experience. You get three minutes to pitch your book to a variety of literary agents and publishers who you signed up to see in advance. I was meeting with a publisher when it hit me. Instead of pitching my book, I asked him, "Could you look around the room and tell me which agent you would trust to bring you a good business book?" Without hesitation he said, "John Willig." Unfortunately, I was not signed up to see him. I jumped into his line anyway and, with the help of a few authors who gave me "cuts," I made it to the front. John understood the concept immediately, and I got an amazing agent. I am truly grateful for his help and efforts in finding my book a place with Career Press. In today's world, many publishers will not take a chance on an unknown author. Career Press did, and Ron Fry's team has been great in welcoming me to the world of publishing, offering guidance and support. Thanks to Michael Pye, Laurie Kelly-Pye, Adam Schwartz, Howard Grossman and Jeff Piasky (love the cover), Roger Sheety, Gina Talucci, and Kirsten Dalley. I hope this is the first of many projects we work on together.

There are others I want to acknowledge. Without my big customers and fellow small business owners, there would be no book. Every person I contacted to provide content said yes, and was generous with his and her time. I don't even know how to thank all of the people at Herman Miller who I have worked with through the years. Herman Miller was my first big customer, and they remain among my favorite people. Siemens, Inc. has also been a wonderful partner, and my thanks go to Carl Oberland. Jim Dunlap and Huntington Bank are my customers, and I am a customer of theirs. That's a true partnership. Thanks to Bob Fish, Heidi Hennink-Kaminski, John Kowalski, Marilyn Landis, Mark Peters, and Rachael Price for all their stories.

I did not even know Christopher Locke, but he responded to an e-mail for help and was a great resource. Others who provided assistance and content include Lynn Afendoulis, Michelle Bottrall, Christa Bird, and Sheila VanZile.

My thanks to all, you know how much you mean to me.

CONTENTS

FOREWORD

Throughout the past 25 years, at regular intervals, Cynthia Kay and her crew would show up to film me and others at Herman Miller for our monthly business reviews— an internal communication video for employees. Herman Miller is a wonderful place to work. It is a global company that designs and creates award-winning products and services for environments where people live, work, learn, and heal. 2012 was a banner year. Herman Miller achieved its ninth consecutive listing on the Dow Jones Sustainability World Index. We were listed among *IndustryWeek* magazine's 50 Best Manufacturing Companies, and inducted into the "Made in USA Hall of Fame" for our commitment to U.S. manufacturing.

In 2011, Herman Miller was designated as one of 10 design icons in *Fast Company*'s "Thirty Companies That Get it" and one of the Top Ten Most Trustworthy Public Companies by Trust Across America. That same year, the company achieved its 23rd year as an industry leader in *FORTUNE* magazine's "Most Admired" companies survey. One very large reason is the nature of the creative network we have had since the 1930s—product designers, graphic designers, researchers, communications groups, and architects. They have helped make Herman Miller a flexible, creative, and open community that has endured for more than 100 years.

Cynthia Kay has become part of that network. Her creativity, drive, and not-so-common competence has made a real contribution to me and to Herman Miller. Her book explores many of the reasons she was able to make such a lasting difference.

"CK," as many people here call her, can be a little pushy. She is certainly confident—that's because she knows what she's doing. What I like best about Cynthia is that she's always pushing *us* to get to the next level. That's the kind of partner/consultant we want at Herman Miller. That's why I agreed to write this foreword. There are lots of books written about business—too many, without anything new to say. This is one I actually read and can heartily recommend.

Why? The force of Cynthia's character, and her ability to tell the truth bluntly, makes *Small Business for Big Thinkers* interesting and profitable for the reader. Cynthia's judgment and experience have tested the lessons in this book. Believe me; I have often turned myself over to her expertise with consistently high results.

Part of the pleasure in reading this book comes from watching her acknowledge the mistakes that many of us make in starting and running a business. And if you remember only a fraction of the insights Cynthia writes about, your business and your life will be better for it.

—Brian Walker, president and
CEO, Herman Miller, Inc.

Introduction

Broadcaster to Business Owner: How I Started Thinking Big

This book is based upon my experience as the owner of a small business that has attracted some large customers. It's an award-winning media production and communication company. But my experience in business began long before I started the company; it began in the backroom of a dry cleaning establishment. It was a family-owned business operated by three brothers, the descendants of Greek immigrants. The brothers also owned a small burger joint right next door where the specialty was—what else?—Greek chili dogs.

I can remember working at the cleaners from the time I was old enough to follow directions. My dad was the middle brother and the only one of the three with a college education.

Every Saturday he would take my sister, younger brother, and me to the store. While he did paperwork, or caught up on loads of clothing in need of attention, we would check in the dirty clothes, put paper inserts on hangers, and clean the store. That was my first foray into business and, believe me, there was no better feeling than having the run of the store. As I got older, I worked my way up to being a counter girl, my first sales experience. Then I was able to open and close the place, my first management experience.

My parents were definitely ahead of their time. In an era when most Greek parents wanted their daughters to "get married and have babies" (yes, that famous line from *My Big Fat Greek Wedding* is very accurate), my parents wanted us to go to school, get educated, and have careers. But, to be clear, my dad did not want us to go into the family business; he wanted us to achieve more. So we did.

My sister, Vicki, went into retailing and today, along with her husband Charles, owns a boutique rental company in Raleigh, North Carolina. They are small, but they do big business. You'll hear more about them throughout this book. My brother, Steve, is a successful litigation and entertainment lawyer, and his wife Bess is a dentist. As for me, I went to Michigan State University, became a broadcaster, and then got my Master's Degree. No over-achievers in this family.

For more than 10 years, I had a successful, award-winning career in broadcast journalism. I did it all; from anchoring, producing, directing, and hosting specialty programming to investigative reporting, documentaries, and features. In the process, I was honored with more than 30 awards from

United Press International, the Associated Press, and numerous regional and local broadcast awards. Pardon the bragging, but you'll see why it is necessary when you read Chapter 14. I got tired of working for a TV station where the owners changed every year or so—and so did the priorities! Every new owner seemed more focused on cost cutting, and less concerned about the quality of the product and the needs of the local community. By the way, I got fired, but that is a topic for a whole other book.

It was time to make a change. I had chances to move to stations in larger markets. But every opportunity I explored seemed like I would be doing the same job, just in a different city. Where was the challenge in that? Like countless others, I dreamed about having more control over my life and career. I wanted to own my own business, run it, and grow it. That's why I founded Cynthia Kay and Company, and in 25 years the business has thrived.

While the company originally served businesses in Michigan, I knew that to survive the economic roller coaster, I needed to attract big businesses throughout the country. I set about working to do just that. Today, CK & Co. serves corporations from the Global Fortune 100, as well as small businesses and non-profit organizations. Our clients are pretty impressive, including Herman Miller, Inc., Siemens Industry, Inc., Dematic, Wiley Publishing, Nestle, affiliates of Susan G. Komen for the Cure, and countless others.

The strategies I am about to share are a major reason for our success. It's a simple but often misunderstood fact. A small business is not just a scaled down version of a big business. Some of the strategies which work well for larger companies may actually be counterproductive for smaller firms.

Small Business for Big Thinkers provides proven strategies to run a better small business that are unconventional, yet logical, clear, understandable, and easy to act upon. The early chapters help lay the foundation for what it takes to build and grow a small business that is healthy, efficient, and a great place to work. If you don't get this right, you simply won't be prepared to work with sophisticated, large customers. Strategies like "Be Ahead of the Pack, But Not *Too* Far Ahead" (Chapter 9), or "Know When It's Time for Employees to Go" (Chapter 10), help position your business so that you can go after big business. In the later chapters, the book provides a roadmap for small companies looking to expand their businesses by *doing* business with *big* business. Trust me; it isn't as easy as it sounds. "The Big Business Buyer's Perspective" (Chapter 12), "How to Get Face-time and When to Show Up" (Chapter 15), along with "Give Something Away, Get More Business" (Chapter 16), show you how to connect and deepen the relationship with large customers. Each chapter ends with Tips to Get You Thinking Big.

By sharing my own experiences, from growing up in a family business to running my own media production company, along with the experiences of others, I aim to provide the kind of information and inspiration that will help small business owners become big thinkers. A fellow business owner told me that her favorite saying is, "Small businesses are not small because we are too stupid to be big." I agree, and would add that you don't need to have lots of employees and mega-facilities to have a big impact. Read on, and start thinking *big*.

1

Big Business Is Waiting:

Where ARE You?

It seems as though there has always been a love/hate relationship between small business and big business. Big businesses get tired of being called slow and inefficient. They hate it when small business is called the backbone of the American economy, the engine that will pull the country out of difficult economic times. Small business owners will tell you that big business gets all the breaks, special treatment, and legislation to help them compete. They say everyone only talks about being a friend of small business. Year after year, politicians give speeches about the importance of small business to job creation and innovation, but many do nothing to help reduce the tax burdens and regulations.

While there is some truth to all of that, here are the facts. According to the Small Business Administration (SBA), there are 27.9 million small businesses in the United States, and they make up 99.7 percent of U.S. employer firms. These businesses employ about 50 percent of the country's private sector workforce.[1] And small business is one of the few sectors that is growing and creating jobs. When most of us think about a small business we think about a local retailer, a restaurant owner, a service provider, or a small manufacturing company. But the true definition of a small business, according to the SBA, is "one with either fewer than 500 employees or net assets under a specific dollar amount of after tax net income for the previous two years."[2] There is also a classification called the "micro business." That is a company that has nine or fewer employees.

No matter what the size of the small business, I have found them to be fiercely proud that they are small. But here is something else I have observed. Many small businesses don't take the time to study their target market. If they did, they might find that big business is where they should concentrate some of their efforts, and they should not wait to get started.

Why big businesses like small businesses

Big businesses were my very first customers, so I never realized until recently that many small businesses don't know how to do business with them. In fact, many small businesses never even try to connect with and win big business. Yes, it can be tricky to navigate the complexities of their purchasing systems, the layers of management, and sometimes confusing practices. But believe it or not, big businesses like small businesses. Why? It's quite simple.

▫ **We are easy to do business with.** We are not likely to have a whole legal staff that wants to negotiate every single point of a contract. We don't have complicated processes and procedures that have to be researched and adhered to.

▫ **We respond quickly.** Our organizations are flexible. We can move schedules around, assign people to step in when needed, and we don't have an 8 a.m. to 5 p.m. mentality. If you need us, we are there, sometimes 24/7.

▫ **We can change course when needed without having to consult endless gatekeepers.** If the scope of a project changes, we adapt. If we need to buy equipment or inventory to accommodate a change, we don't have to wait to get approvals which might stall the work.

▫ **We bring them great new ideas.** We love to create new things instead of doing things the way they have always been done. We get excited by new challenges.

▫ **We believe that we can make things happen, so we do.** My favorite phrase is "it is doable." We find ways to pull off even the most difficult projects.

▫ **Finally, because we are "lean," we provide a great value and don't waste their time or money.** Small business owners spend their client's money as if it was their own. I routinely advise my big clients that they are asking me to do something that will cost them money unnecessarily. They appreciate that.

For all of these reasons, and many more, big businesses like to work with small business. At least, that's what I think. But I decided to test my theory out on a few of my big customers, fellow small business owners, and others. Many of those I reached out to have worked for both large and small businesses.

Bigger is not necessarily better

Marilyn Landis is one small business owner who understands both sides of the small business/big business landscape. She worked for three of the largest Small Business Association lenders in the country. She currently runs her own small business, Basic Business Concepts, Inc., and serves on the Board of the National Small Business Association. Landis says:

> Some businesses function best as small businesses, but that does not mean we are not very sophisticated or that we don't have very complex systems. We are sophisticated, and we do have systems in place to help us deliver flawlessly. There is a saying that I love: "those who think bigger is better and older is smarter, forget the dinosaur that got bigger, not better, and older, not smarter."[3]

Attention and flexibility get you noticed

John Kowalski, director of strategic marketing for a global manufacturing company, has been my client for many years, both with his current company, and at a previous one as well. John has a unique perspective because he is also the owner of a small consulting company. As a result, he too sees both sides of the story. In his role with a large manufacturing company, he has a number of small businesses as service suppliers. When asked why he prefers them to some of the big guys, he said:

> Smaller suppliers are more attentive, more flexible and, most importantly, they listen. They provide a non–corporate America perspective of things. When you are on the inside of a big corporation, it is easy to get tainted, to get sucked into that corporate mindset. I want something to make my project better. As a result, I want a different perspective, and a smaller company can often provide that.[4]

Of course, this is not true of all small businesses. But it is true of those that are well-run and forward-thinking.

Another reason big companies like small companies is the expertise and availability of the owner. Kowalski says:

> With a big company you get the sales person or the account executive in to make the sale, then you never see them again. It's, 'Here, I'll take that signed contract, and Bob over there will take care of you.' And Bob is generally someone with a lot less experience than the person that sold me the job. I don't want to train someone. I want an expert. When I work with a small company, I get the owner and their support staff. I am getting *the* experts in that firm. The owner or managing partner has their hand in every aspect of that company. They are going to direct the work

and make sure it is right. After all, their name is on the door.[5]

In my first interview for a contract with a large manufacturing company, I was a little put off by the questions. The interviewer kept asking, "And who will do the interviewing, and who will be on site, and who will I communicate with?" To every question I answered, "That would be me!" I found out later that this individual had been burned. The previous supplier did exactly what John Kowalski described above. They got the contract and then sent in junior level employees to do the work and, I might add, not very successfully.

Small businesses love to experiment

In addition to working directly with the business owner, big businesses like the entrepreneurial spirit of small companies. They like that we will experiment with them. Mark Peters, CEO of Butterball Farms, Inc., began his career working for a large company and now works with some of the biggest names in fast-food chains, as well as major food producers. His company is the largest national dairy supplier of specialty and premium butter in the U.S., but it is still a small business. Peters says:

> There's a lot more at stake for us as small business owners because once you get the business, you can't afford to lose it. Years ago, we were willing to do an experiment for a leading global food service retailer with restaurants in approximately 199 countries. They were concerned about running out of product. We were concerned about balancing the production

level in our plant. So we invested some time and money and became the pilot for a whole new Vendor Managed Inventory system that they ended up implementing. We were their first U.S. supplier to do that. Everyone benefitted. We reaped huge benefits by being able to level load our production plant, and schedule our own shipments. We got rid of a ton of overtime. We also were able to give our customer what they needed, a reliable supply of product. By delivering what they need, when they need it, we reduce the risk of losing their business.[6]

Are you ready to do big business?

So how do you know if doing business with big business is right for you? Here are a few things to ask yourself and your team before you start to court big business.

- **Are you ready for a new challenge?** Doing business with a large company won't be the same as working with smaller customers. Big customers have very different needs and expect a high level of performance.

- **Are you are more forward-thinking than your current customers?** Big businesses are always looking for those who can help them get ahead and give them a fresh, outside perspective, especially during tough economic times.

- **Can you ramp up your capacity if you get a huge contract?** Getting the contract is just the start. You have a lot of hard work ahead of you after that.

◻ **Do you have the machinery, space, people, etc., to deal with spikes in business?** You will need to find the money to make investments and have great cash flow to help you deal with the ups and downs, not to mention many big businesses take a while to pay.

◻ **Do you have the technology you need?** You can't be behind in this area. Big business does not have the time to wait while you figure this out.

◻ **Do you have a product or service that you have perfected?** You have to be the best at what you do because you are unproven and they are looking for a quality product.

◻ **Do you know how to build long-lasting relationships?** Big business does not want to spend time and money getting you into their system and educating you about their business for a one-time job. Many have been trying to reduce their supplier base and consolidate suppliers.

◻ **Are you willing to do what it takes?** The truth is, big business is demanding. So be really clear on this one.

This is just the start of it. Doing business with big business is not for everyone. I know small business owners who actually lost money on jobs. One owner told me that a huge contract caused them to staff up only to have to lay people off when the contract was not renewed. Another said they had to grow so fast that the quality of their work suffered. You have to be ready for these contingencies.

So what do I mean when I say big business is waiting? It's no surprise that big businesses have had a rough go of it. They have down-sized, and now many of them find themselves with staff that is overburdened. They may not have invested a lot in their operations or their people due to economic conditions, so they have to play catch-up. Or, on a more positive note, they may be working to launch new products or services, and are seeking out the best suppliers to help them.

One example of how big business is working to help promote small business is Supplier Connection. Six major corporations have come together to launch a supplier initiative that is aimed at helping small businesses market themselves to large companies. It's a free Web-based portal, *www.supplierconnection.net*, which provides small companies a chance to register basic information and share business practices. Large company buyers can use the portal to find small business suppliers that they might want to hire. I believe this effort really highlights the recognition by large companies that small business is critically important to the economy and new job creation. These large companies are not just waiting for small businesses to find them, they are proactive.

In short, this is a time of opportunity, but only if you get operationally efficient, creative, and pay attention. The journey to connecting with and winning big business starts before you even open the doors and continues by running the best possible small business operation.

TIPS TO GET YOU THINKING BIG

- Don't wait to start researching potential big business customers.

- There are many things that big businesses like about small businesses, including responsiveness, flexibility, and creativity.

- Use the checklist in this chapter to see if you are ready to do business with big business.

- Big business is reaching out. Check out the Supplier Connection.

2

HAVE AN EXIT STRATEGY
BEFORE YOU OPEN THE DOORS

There is no doubt about it; new small businesses are springing up every day. More people than ever are motivated to pursue the American Dream of opening a small business and being the boss. What's the attraction?

Countless individuals have been downsized out of large companies and, given the economic downturn, have been unable to find employment. Others have simply decided to leave the corporate world to pursue a dream and bet on themselves. The acceleration of the Internet and e-commerce has made it easier than ever to launch a business with a minimal investment. But in the rush to open the doors, many miss one important step: they forget to think about an exit strategy. This is not uncommon. Most business owners love their business. Why else would they have started it or purchased it? They love the excitement of creating something, the rush when someone buys their product or when they land a big account. Exit strategy? Why would you even want to think about it?

Simple: if you know how you want to exit, it will help determine how you build, operate, and run your small business. In addition, having a plan and a sound structure in place shows your big business customers that you have taken care of business. That is very important if you want to be a long-term partner with big business clients.

Questions to get you thinking about exiting

There are several questions you need to ask yourself when formulating an exit strategy. They may sound elementary, but getting crystal clear about the answers will help you decide on an ordered exit.

- What are your long-term plans for the business, assuming that you make it through those first rough years?
- Do you want partners?
- Do you want to grow the business, or stay small and keep your hands in all aspects of the operation?
- Are you thinking about growing the business quickly so you can sell it?
- What would it take for you to sell your business? How much money? What kind of a deal?

- Have you looked into the type of buyer that would be interested in your business?

- Do you want to work until you are well past the age when most people retire? Or, do you want to retire early? (Good luck with that one.)

- Do you want to leave your business to the next generation? Is there a family member that might be a likely buyer or manager?

- Do you want to turn your business into a franchise? If you do, how will that change your role?

Knowing what you want drives the decisions you make and the timing of your exit. Believe me—exiting from a small business can be complicated. Here are a few examples from my own experience.

Exiting a family-owned business

My father's business, Afendoulis Cleaners, was owned by three brothers. It started like many family businesses—no business plan, no buy-sell agreements, and no job descriptions—just a lot of hard work, some intuition, and a bit of luck. Some would say it's a wonder that the family survived the building of the business, several downturns in the economy, and the buy-out of first one brother and then another, especially considering there was no exit strategy. Like many business owners, the brothers thought that one of the children would step up. That was probably the exit strategy, but there was nothing written down.

When it came time for my dad to retire, it was difficult. He did not want to leave this wonderful business that was so much a part of his life, but he could see what was happening. He was getting older and had some health issues. His brother wanted to keep working and had a son-in-law who had recently moved back to town. My siblings and I did not want the business. Dad wanted to sell the business and the property, and have both brothers retire. His brother wanted to keep working. It is not uncommon that people have different timetables given their age, health, and other family dynamics.

It was time to negotiate an exit and, without an agreement in place, that is not easy. Everyone thinks they are entitled to more. Everyone thinks their contribution to the enterprise was the reason for its success. The truth is probably somewhere in the middle. In this case, each brother wanted to be sure they gave the other brother his due.

I remember the day my dad retired. I stood with him behind the well-worn counter of the dry-cleaning store as he reminisced about the business, his customers, things he should have done but did not. In many ways, he was torn because he did not want to leave. At the same time, he knew that he had to. Many of his favorite customers had stopped by during the afternoon to wish him well. When all were gone, I took his hand and gently guided him out the door.

This was one of those rare moments when he cried. I think the negotiations had been difficult. But it is a testament to the character of the individuals who started the business and our families that, to this day, the relationships are intact. Often, that is not the case.

A lesson learned

As much as I saw the pitfalls of business partnerships (that's a whole other lesson we'll cover later), I still thought I needed someone to complement my talents when I started my business. So I found a partner. I knew from observing our family's business that I needed a plan and the legal documents. The buy-sell was one of the first things we addressed so we would have an exit strategy. I thought it was important that it not be a 50/50 deal. Someone needed to be the lead. I was taking on a greater financial risk by using the equity in my house as collateral, so it was decided I would own 51 percent of the business, and my partner would own 49 percent. For a number of years, things went along well. Then, over time, it became obvious that we were simply not on the same path. He wanted to keep the business small, really small, and exert lots of control over every aspect of it. I wanted to grow the business—not too big—but big enough so that we could attract the type of big clients and projects that would keep it interesting. I also knew that I did not want to be one of those business owners that had no work-life balance. However, without the extra bodies, I knew that I would have to do everything. I could not focus on attracting new business, and moving the company forward with new products and services.

To try and reconcile our differences, my partner and I went to business counseling. We worked with a consultant for a number of sessions to see if we could find that common ground that we had when we started the business. It worked for a while, but soon things were right back to where we started before our attempts to save the partnership.

In the beginning, I felt that my partner and I had our differences, but we were essentially headed down the same path. As time went on, that was less and less the case. I decided, after a lot of pain and anguish, that I no longer wanted to be in business with him. The options were simple: I buy him out, he buys me out, or we sell the whole thing. That last option was the least desirable because it would have taken far too long to find a buyer and make the transition. When we set up the business, we put a buy-sell agreement in place. Because there was an exit strategy, it took about 80 days from start to finish.

I bought him out, and decided to sit tight and run the business. We were very transparent with both employees and customers about what we were doing. In fact, we discussed early on that, no matter who was making the exit, we would communicate jointly to our big customers. We did not want to risk losing business, so we set up meetings and told them of our plan. It worked. In the long run, I knew I had made the right decision not to be the one taking leave. Of course, I have continued to invest in it. That investment, along with growing the client base consisting of bigger customers, has made the business more valuable. Now I'm working on the more long-term exit strategy.

The options for exiting a small business are varied. If you decide to sell the business, you need to have a plan. This will take some study, soul-searching, and a lot of time.

Consider your options

Family-owned businesses have different ways of passing the business down from generation to generation. Is there a group of employees that might have an interest? I know of several small businesses that have set up Employee Stock Ownership Plans (ESOP) which provide employees stock, often at no cost to them. While this might be a great option, it can also be a little pricey for a small business to set up and administer.

You can bring in a younger employee, train him or her, and do a buyout over time. This helps make the transition easier for customers. It may also make the deal more attractive to banks or other lenders, because the individual has knowledge of the business and has already made an investment.

If there is no one on staff that has an interest in buying, you might choose to use a business broker. Depending upon the size and complexity of your business, you may be able to initially make these connections on your own. If you need anonymity, then you will want to use an outside source.

Is there a competitor that could benefit by acquiring your operation? Or, is there a related business that could add to their product and service offering by merging their business with yours? Consider all the options carefully, and don't be afraid to ask other business owners about plans that they have considered. They may be willing to share ideas and strategies that have worked well or failed.

No exit strategy: Is that a strategy?

There is one strategy that I have not explored. It's having no exit strategy. Bob Fish is the CEO and co-founder of Biggby Coffee, one of the top 20 food service franchise concepts in the nation. He says that he has no exit strategy:

I don't have one because I don't intend on exiting. I'm not racing to some IPO [initial public offering] just so that I can rally up the stock price and get out. I am building a company for the long haul. We have had many offers to be bought, and we've entertained some of those, but we've never been interested in selling. This is not what I do so that I can have a hobby. I have built my life and my job to be intertwined so that I can still spend a lot of time with my family, pursuing other interests like travel and personal development. I really believe in a balanced lifestyle. Occasionally that gets tested. It has to be a little elastic. But what I'd like to do is build a company that survives me, and I only have so much time left on this earth to do that. My goal is not to figure out my exit strategy, but to figure out how to ensure that the company survives me. That's my legacy.[1]

After hearing that and seeing firsthand the passion that Fish has for his company, I think that not having an exit strategy is also a strategy. While I really like the idea of a company living on—and I want that same thing for my company—you have to put a lot of thought into how to make that happen. You will need a solid business model and trusted people at various levels of the company to "work it," because the reality is that most people just can't keep working at the same pace as they move into their later years. Of course, there is always an exception and Bob Fish might be one. But none of us will live forever, so you will need to work with legal counsel to handle how to pass on the shares or ownership of the company, sell it, or simply liquidate the assets.

Know when to re-evaluate

Exit strategies vary widely and you may need to change your plan over the years. Maybe you thought you would retire at 65, but your retirement account took a hit and now you need to work longer. Maybe some big company loves your product and wants to buy you out. Perhaps, like my friend Bob Fish, you find that you just love to work and can't imagine the day when you get up and don't have a place to go. The simple fact is that, no matter how much you love your potential or current business, there will come a time that you need to reevaluate your options. Here are a few questions you should ask yourself:

- Do you want to continue to run the business and work for five or 10 more years?
- Should you think about selling because the company is profitable?
- Do you have interest from motivated buyers who might go away if you delay a sale?
- Should you merge with another company?
- Is it time to pass it on to the next generation?
- Is it best to sell the assets and close the doors?

The one thing I have noticed among fellow business owners is the tendency to let their businesses get out of shape and sloppy when they decide to sit tight. I think that is because they are trying to milk as much as they can out of the company without investing too much more. What's the problem? When you let the business get old and tired, you start to lose customers, especially big ones who do business with you because you are forward-thinking and aggressive. Key employees see the lack of attention and start to worry about the future. They often pick up and move to a place that has more potential and a more secure outlook. When a business starts to decline, it is not easy to reverse the trend. So if you decide to sit tight, pay attention or you might not get those few extra years of income because it simply won't be there.

Timing your exit

It may seem odd to talk about selling your business and timing your exit so early in this book, but you need to have a vision. One business owner I know had no intention of selling her business, but interested parties kept contacting her on behalf of individuals looking to buy businesses. She looked at a few offers but just could not get comfortable with the idea. There were a number of reasons, but foremost amongst them was that she was still in the growth phase and knew that the work she was doing would pay off. There were several large long-term contracts in the works that would keep them busy for years and add to the value of the business. The following year, an interested buyer returned and increased the offer more than a million dollars. She still did not want to sell and, to this day, is running the business. She had to add staff and warehouse space, but the timing was just not right for her to exit.

Of course, the opposite can happen as well. Your business can be very profitable for a period of time and then can start to decline. If you did not sell during those good years, you may have to take less money. Many individuals sold businesses in 2012 because the timing was just right. The changes in the tax codes made it attractive to sell and pay less capital gains taxes, so there was a flurry of buying and selling activity. We may not see that again for many years.

But timing an exit is not just about the money. There are many personal reasons that prompt an exit, including failing health. The Baby Boomer generation is now caring for aging parents, and the struggle to do that and run a business can be overwhelming. It's a balancing act. The best case scenario is to have a steady and predictable financial picture so that you can choose when to exit and realize the best possible situation—both financially and personally.

Should you close the doors?

Another option for exiting a business is to just close the doors. While this seems drastic, it happens time and time again. There are a number of factors that influence this decision. I have seen businesses that can no longer afford the space they rented due to increases in rent or lack of sales. One business closed up shop because it had invested too much in the development of a new product that never launched. I know of another small business that lost a major client, more than 60 percent of their sales, and that was enough to force them to shut down. Diversification is paramount. But many ignore this reality, lose an important client, and then must make the decision to close the doors before the expenses start to pile up.

A few final thoughts

If you are a sole proprietor in a service business, you are especially vulnerable. You are the business. You have the relationships and deliver the service. If you can no longer work, there is really nothing to sell except goodwill or a list, and that just does not go very far.

If you're starting a business, be sure you think about an exit strategy and know that it might change over time. If you own a business and do not have a strategy, it's not too late—start now. If you have a strategy but it no longer makes good business sense, revisit it and develop a new one that does.

Here's one final story that illustrates the point. A number of years ago I got a call from a senior executive at a large company. I had been working with him that day and was surprised to hear from him. He told me that he had put in his notice that afternoon. I could not imagine why he wanted to quit. He had a great job, seemed to be at the top of his game, and had just successfully completed one of the biggest projects of his career. I did not think anyone was pushing him out and he confirmed that. So why leave?

For some of the reasons I just mentioned. He was at the top of his game, and he wanted to leave on his own terms and his own timeframe. He wanted to be in control of his exit. When you work for someone else, control is often difficult. When you own your own business, you have control, but only if you have an exit strategy.

TIPS TO GET YOU
THINKING BIG

▢ When you start to plan an exit strategy, get legal assistance and don't skimp. A good lawyer saves you time and money in the long run.

▢ If you decide to form a partnership, remember that they are difficult even under the best circumstances, so choose wisely.

▢ Create a detailed exit strategy with a number of scenarios and reevaluate them regularly.

▢ Let key customers and employees know what you are doing. Don't surprise them with big organizational changes; it makes them very nervous.

3

GET SMART ABOUT PARTNERING: CREATE A BUSINESS PRENUP

Growing up in a family-owned business, I witnessed the importance of what I call a "business prenup." Sometimes the business worked wonderfully; other times, it was chaotic. The chaos existed because there was no real understanding about what each partner brought to the table and how the partnership would work. There were no agreements in place. So, when it came time for one of the partners to "divorce," the split-up was sometimes painful—financially and emotionally.

When entrepreneurs go into business, they often struggle with this dilemma: partner-up or buy the talent you need to get started. Many do what I did and make the leap with a partner. Some might wonder why I thought I needed a partner. Actually, there were many times over the course of the partnership that I asked myself, "What were you thinking?" I could say I wasn't thinking, but that would not be honest. My business is a media production and communications consulting company. It has some very definite areas of expertise; there is the creative part and the technical side. I have always been good at the creative aspect, and I have some technical ability as well. But I did not think that I had enough expertise to handle all the changes in technology that are so much a part of this business. That's why I decided to partner up; I thought it would be a good blend of talents. I chose someone that I worked with at a TV station. We started freelancing together and it worked well. So when I decided to open the business, it seemed like a logical move because we had worked together informally. At the time, I thought I knew him fairly well from a business standpoint, but we did not have the kind of conversations that I now know are critical to any business relationship. The truth is, you never really know how someone will react in a business setting until you are there together working down in the trenches.

How a business prenup differs from the traditional prenup

Many people today go into a marriage with a prenuptial agreement. Why? Because they know that there are always negative things that can happen and they want to protect themselves. Prenuptial agreements vary widely, but they usually include provisions for support: how you will divide property, grounds for forfeiture of assets, and so on.

When you have a partner you need to properly define the business issues: structure, percent of ownership, buy-out conditions, etc. This needs to be done very early in the process of starting a business. It is tricky and delicate, as delicate as asking your fiancé for a prenuptial agreement. Does it mean you think the venture will fail? Do you not trust your partner? Or are you simply being realistic?

Of course, there are the typical areas to address. What if someone wants out? What if one partner is no longer able to work for health reasons? How will you evaluate the worth of the business? What happens in the case of bankruptcy? But there are other personal issues that you need to address that are not usually part of some legal agreement. These are the fuzzy, gray areas that pop up because everyone has their own unique personality, style of working, and values. This is where my concept of the business prenup goes beyond the typical things you think of with traditional agreements. Here are a few things to consider.

Get personal and ask questions

When developing a business prenup, you need to set aside some time to ask each other a number of questions. This is not a single conversation, but a series of conversations. Take notes; then you can go back and refer to them later to see if they resonate after the discussion. Here are some of the areas to address:

- What do you know about the person's family, background, and values? They say that business is business, but it's also personal and that is influenced greatly by family.

- Do you have personalities that complement each other?

- Do you want to spend time with this person? You will see them more than you see your own family.

- Do either of you have problems with anger, such as passive, aggressive behavior? No one is likely to tell you this, so you have to be observant. This is one that can cost you big customers, issues with employees, and legal bills when things get out of hand.

- Will a spouse or significant other be involved in the business? If so, who calls the shots?

- What is your idea of work-life balance? Does it match your partner's perspective?

- Does anything about the person bother you? Do they talk too much? Do they seem too controlling? Are they too easy-going?

- Do they socialize with people that make you uncomfortable? Do they engage in risky behavior?

- Have they ever been in trouble, even as a child (which won't be on their record)?

- Are they good communicators? This is one point that many people discount, yet is one of the most important. If your partner does not communicate with you frequently and effectively, you will find yourself in the middle of situations you did not anticipate. Then you end up in a reactive mode, instead of a proactive one.

◻ Do they pay attention to their health and wellness? Is their lifestyle a healthy one?

◻ Do they coast through situations, avoiding confrontation?

◻ Do they tell lies (even little white ones), or exaggerate the truth?

◻ Do they have a positive outlook, or are they more focused on the negative?

◻ Are they solution-oriented or problem-oriented?

◻ Do they have a sense of humor? Are they able to laugh at themselves and not take themselves too seriously?

◻ Do they make excuses for things that go wrong or take responsibility?

◻ Are they willing to ask for help?

I left this one for last because it is so important. When you are a small business owner, and thinking big, you simply can't know it all. You have to rely on trusted advisors, peers, and others to help you navigate difficult situations. If you can't ask for help, you are doomed to make mistakes. Watch carefully to see if your potential partner is a know-it-all or has developed the habit of reaching out for assistance.

Ask business-related questions

Once you have gotten through all the personal prenup questions, it is time to get down to more specifically business-related points:

◻ How big do you want to grow the business?

◻ What kind of customers do you want to connect with and win? If your partner is afraid of big businesses, and some are, you will not be able to capture that market.

◻ How will you make hiring decisions? What if you don't agree about whether to hire or who to hire?

◻ How much financial risk are you comfortable with?

◻ Who will be your outside resources and what will they do? Some business owners insist on doing activities that are better left to outside resources. If you end up with a partner that is a "do-it-yourselfer," it can get you in real trouble. This is especially important when it comes to the legal and accounting areas. Laws and requirements change all the time. If you don't have professionals to help keep you up to date, you may find yourself paying fines or worse.

◻ What will be a typical work week? This can cause issues if one person feels like they are putting more time into the business than the other.

◻ How much money should be reinvested in the business?

◻ How will you decide on salary adjustments? Will you both be paid equally or should you get paid on the value of the work? Is one type of work more important than another?

◻ What will you do when you disagree?

◻ How will you reward employees?

◻ Until what age do you want to work?

◻ How much will you donate to charity, and how will you decide who to support?

Throughout the years that I had a partner, each and every one of these questions caused an issue. Sometimes it was a minor conversation, others times it was a huge fight. As I have mentioned, at one point, my partner and I even went to business counseling. The situation that brought it to a head was the decision to hire an additional person so that we could take on more work. My partner did not want to let go of some of his responsibilities. In fact, he did not want to share his knowledge with our employees so that they could take on more responsibility, freeing us up to do higher-level work. He wanted control of every aspect of the business. This meant that we simply could not continue to grow. It became obvious to me that our vision for the business did not match. In truth, I knew that there would be differences of opinion, but I never thought it would reach the point where one of us had to leave.

When that time came, I knew I had to make the transition happen. I was open to being the one who had to go. As it worked out, I stayed and he went. That opened up a whole new avenue for the business. I made many adjustments, hired people, invested in equipment, and sought out new customers. It took a while, but all of these efforts have made the business even more successful.

A story of three sisters

Some stories about partnerships are far more positive than mine. Take, for example, the three sisters, Becky, Rachael and Kate, who own Tre Bella Inc., a company that started out as a small florist working out of the home of one of the sisters. Almost 10 years later, the company is a full service floral and bridal salon with an impeccable reputation for quality and creativity. That's why Tre Bella has outgrown two facilities. When the sisters decided to go into business one lived in Colorado, another in Washington DC and the third in North Carolina. Rachael Price says, "We did a lot of research. When I was out in Boulder I went around to different florists and met with lots of industry experts. We took seminars and I actually did an internship with a florist in our hometown."[1]

The sisters did a great job of setting up the business and, by all accounts, have figured out how to use the differences in their personalities and skill sets to their advantage. As Rachael Price says:

> It was sort of an evolution of figuring it out over time, who worked best in what role. I don't think we could have done it, or would have done it, on our own. I believe having a partner can be really good because when I can't be there, there is an owner that cares as much as I do about the customer. Of course, you have to be very upfront with each other about your expectations. I think that's what we've learned over the years. We didn't do that initially, and I think it took us several years to figure it out. I think it would've made it easier if we would have discussed even more things at the beginning.[2]

Some believe that it is best to have an uneven number of partners. That way it is easier to take a vote and make a decision. While partnering with family might not sound ideal to some, for these three sisters it has been successful. Rachael says:

If you have a partner, it is easier to walk away when things don't go well. But we are sisters, and it has worked to hold our business together. It's inevitable; if you're sisters or just business partners, you're going to have arguments. That's because you are making big decisions. At the end of the day, we work very hard to separate things out. Business is business and family is family. So when we vote and a decision is made, we move on.[3]

A final thought

The decision to partner-up is one that can bring you great joy and security, like the three sisters, or it can lead to huge issues. I think back on my decision to partner-up and believe I should have paid much more attention to the business prenup. I should have asked the questions, and then really listened and observed to see if the answers added up. Sometimes we hear what we want to hear—that is exactly what I did. I did not pay attention to the personal and business prenup. I should have been smarter about partnering up. The buy-sell agreement did make it easier to get out, but if I had paid more attention to the list of questions, I wouldn't have started the business with a partner. I would have gone it alone or found someone more suitable. Today I know that I could have made it alone because I do have the skill set needed and can get the talent to fill in the gaps, as I have done since my "business divorce."

TIPS TO GET YOU THINKING BIG

◻ If you are thinking about partnering up, set aside some time to ask both business and personal questions.

◻ Take notes or record the conversation so that you can both hear it back later.

◻ Consider getting some outside assistance to facilitate the discussion before you partner up.

◻ Talk to other business owners who have partners. Ask them to share with you the good, the bad, and the ugly about partnerships, so you can be prepared.

◻ Revisit the business prenup every few years. You need to be prepared, because things change and people change.

◻ Don't be afraid to go it alone and hire the skill set you need.

4

FIND THE MONEY NEEDED TO LAUNCH AND THE CREDIT TO KEEP GOING

One of the biggest issues that every entrepreneur faces is taking a great idea or product and turning it into a viable business. The issue is M-O-N-E-Y. Quite simply, sometimes no one wants to lend you money when you need it (and maybe with good reason). Naturally, by the time you don't need it, *everyone* wants to lend you money.

The statistics are grim. According to the 2012 National Small Business Association (NSBA) Small Business Access to Capital Survey, "nearly half (43 percent) of small business respondents said that, in the last four years, they needed funds and were unable to find any willing sources, be it loans, credit cards, or investors."[1] So how does this lack of capital affect small business? Think about it. You can't launch the business or new initiative, and you can't expand if you've already started one. You don't even dare to think about hiring more employees, and you might need to lay some employees off. You don't have the money to market your product or services. You might not be able to buy or lease the new equipment you need to meet the requirements of new sales efforts, not to mention purchasing the inventory needed to meet the demand. You may have to close facilities or retail stores. If you are working with big businesses, you will need to be prepared for the reality that many take 90 days to pay you for your services, which may affect your cash flow. (We'll talk more about that later.)

So what do you do? To begin, you need to understand a few of the factors that come into play when you are looking for loans. First, lenders look at what phase of business you are in: start-up, second stage, or mature business. Next, they ask what kind of business you have: manufacturing, professional service, technology, retail, health care, and so on. Finally, what experience do you have that specifically applies to this business? The answers to these questions may lead you in very different directions when trying to access capital. But even in these tough times, there are some options—certainly more than when I went looking for my first loan.

Today, the options are many: venture capital, angel investors, private equity companies, banks, SBA and USDA loans, grants and individual investors, plus non-bank lenders, nonprofit or government economic development agencies, and private lending funds. I am sure there are even more that I have not listed and new ones that are appearing on the scene every day.

The search for funding

I started by researching a Small Business Administration loan. The process, for me, was time consuming and frustrating. The paperwork alone was unbelievable; especially when you consider the fact that I wasn't looking for a huge amount of money—less than $80,000. I know I am not alone. The average balance on a small business loan or line of credit, according to the NSBA Survey, is about $256,000.[2] Many people need much less. So how much paperwork do you really want to do? In fairness, I understand that the SBA has streamlined the process and is working to strengthen their lending programs. But some small business owners don't think that progress is happening quickly enough. So, like me, you may want to look further, especially if you are on a fast track.

As my search for the money to launch the company continued, I was approached by a successful businessman who heard about my venture and offered to invest. Of course, he wanted a good-size piece of the business. Think *Shark Tank*, that popular TV show where entrepreneurs try to get the celebrity panel to invest. Some of the contestants trade a significant piece of their business for cash, others walk away. That's what I did; I walked away and continued the search. This businessman, by today's definition, would be an angel investor. An angel investor is generally an affluent individual who provides backing for a business start-up, usually in exchange for convertible debt or ownership equity. There are also angel groups or angel networks available. These are individuals who get together and pool their dollars, and then invest in business opportunities. This lets them share research on the companies, and theoretically spreads out the risk to all the investors.

A lot of people think that angel investors are the way to go. But some experts I spoke with warn that the vast majority of small businesses have *no business* looking for an angel investor. That's because they cannot pay the kind of returns an angel investor will demand. There are exceptions. One is the start-up that is a cutting edge technology company where there is a great deal of interest, even before the company begins to generate revenue.

I ended up starting my business in a pretty traditional way. I visited several banks and went shopping for a loan. I read all the books about the need for a business plan and then created one. I did my homework and studied the market. I had strong references. I even took my accountant on the calls to the banks so I had back-up. I put together a road show. That's right, a complete presentation designed to dazzle the loan officers. I even had a leave-behind for them with the new company logo. That really did not impress them—I am not sure what I was thinking!

It became clear to me very quickly that not all banks are created equal. Just because you have done business with a bank in the past does not necessarily mean that they will be your best choice now, or that they will even want your loan. I was sure that the bank that I had been doing business with personally would be the first to step up—not so. As it turned out, they did not really like service businesses. They were much more impressed by brick and mortar. I ended up with a bank that had a good relationship with my accountant. All the fancy work I did for the road show was good, because it showed that I did my homework. But what really convinced them to make the loan was the experience I had in my previous job; they thought that would be valuable. Essentially, I had been learning and making mistakes on someone else's dime. I was also fortunate to have had a high-profile media job where I had made a lot of connections. The bank believed I could leverage those connections and turn them into customers.

Another thing in my favor was that my accountant had a great reputation for working with small businesses, so they knew I would have sound financial advice and safeguards in place. Of course, I still had to sign a personal guarantee using the equity in my house. Everything I have ever read, and everyone I talk to, says "don't sign a personal guarantee." You probably don't have a choice; I did not. But, after all, it is the bank's money and I, like most entrepreneurs, believed in the business. I felt that if I wasn't confident enough to take the risk, why should anyone else believe in me? Sure it was a risk, but it was worth taking.

Once I got that first loan, I did something that many entrepreneurs don't think about: I made accelerated payments. Everyone talks about making sure that your payments are on time, but I believe you should do more. When you repay a loan quickly, it gets easier and easier to get the next loan. That is what happened to me, so I encourage business owners to get aggressive and pay down or pay off loans.

Today, getting a loan is a very different story. Banks previously lent money to start-ups based on home equity because they thought it was a less risky investment. The recent recession proved that was not true. If you decide to go the traditional banking route, you need to understand the current economic climate and how banks look at you and your business.

The banker's point of view

I have been fortunate during the past 10 years to have a great relationship with a bank that is friendly toward small business. Small business owners rated Huntington Bank highest in the nation for customer satisfaction with small business banking, according to the J.D. Power and Associates 2012 U.S. Small Business Banking Satisfaction Study.[3] According to Jim Dunlap, senior executive vice president, regional and commercial banking director, small business owners need to be prepared, make a compelling business case and understand what banks are looking for in a relationship. Dunlap says:

> All relationships work most productively when there is something in it for both parties. A business owner comes in and says, "By the way, with this capital injection I can do this," which is, of course, borrowing money. If everything goes perfectly and the bank extends the money and gets paid back right on schedule, we get our interest and our principal back. That's what's in it for us. What's in it for the business owner is all the opportunity they have, multiples of what the bank would make on that loan.[4]

Banks don't get to share in the significant gains that entrepreneurs can achieve with a highly successful project. Their goal is to underwrite a loan where there is the highest probability that they will get the loan paid back with interest.

That's why, according to Dunlap, "The business owner has to make a compelling case. That is not to say that the idea is perfect, in and of itself, but that it will generate the ability for them to pay us back with interest."[5]

Entrepreneurs are dreamers. They are builders. They are just plain excited about their idea or business. What they often forget to consider is the risk that the bank, or any other lender, is taking. That is why the lender asks for both primary and secondary sources of repayment. Dunlap says business owners need to be prepared for a conversation about what might happen if things go terribly wrong, and not be insulted by these questions. Those who have given much thought to the bumps in the road and are prepared with contingency plans are more credible.

Dunlap says, "Let's talk about how we really lose money. We lose money by death, drugs, divorce, and fraud." These are life events that no one really plans for or anticipates. Those kinds of circumstances disrupt all our best intentions. So before those events happen, the bank has to pay attention to how flexible and resilient you are. Dunlap suggests going to the bank and saying, "I have a problem and I want you to know about it early." This gives that banker substantial opportunity and many choices for how to proceed. If you wait too long to tell your banker that there are problems, that is when the real problems occur. As Dunlap says, "At that point, I have to protect the principal investment and that means that I have no choice but to take action."[6]

So here are two key questions to ask yourself before visiting your bank:

1. What's in it for both parties? Is this deal mutually beneficial?

2. Are you prepared if events in your life, or at your business, cause things to go terribly wrong?

These are critical questions. You have to be brutally honest with yourself and your potential lender. Dunlap says:

> When a business owner comes in prepared to answer these questions, their chances for accessing capital are 90 percent better, because the business owner has thought through those things, exposed them to their bank, and is vulnerable enough to talk about them. That gives the banker confidence that this is a different kind of a client and partnership than if you simply just bring us your financials.[7]

There is a difference in how banks underwrite small businesses versus big businesses. According to Dunlap, big businesses are judged by the balance sheet, capital, and experience. Small businesses are viewed a bit differently. Dunlap says:

> We underwrite small businesses based upon the degree of competency and capability of the owners and managers. We will underwrite their business plans a lot more intensely than we would the larger businesses that have capital opportunities that smaller businesses don't. But that does not mean in any way, shape, or form one has an advantage over the other. In fact, if you've got a highly competent management team, a well-thought-out business plan, good

projections that align with that business plan, experience in personal and management skills, then you can have a high degree of confidence we're going to go ahead and invest in you regardless of the size of the company, because these are the things that ultimately help businesses to weather the storms.[8]

One of the common complaints of small business owners is that they believe banks don't like to do business with them because the loan amounts requested are much smaller—sometimes as little as $10,000 to $100,000—and the amount of effort to get the return is too great. Dunlap says there is more to the story:

You put in a certain amount of effort to get a certain amount of return. That is undeniable. However, let me give the compelling alternative to why those small businesses are so incredibly valuable for us. First of all, there is a loyalty factor that small companies demonstrate that large corporations don't. When you bank a small business, you bank that person and everything associated with them. So you have a full investment of that company through their owner, and their managers, and their colleagues. Rarely do you get that in a larger company. They can't declare loyalty. They're not as interested in loyalty as small businesses are, because they know they need those personal relationships to transcend the business relationships. Secondly, concentration of capital matters to us just like it does for a private investor. I would rather have 50 small business investments than two large ones and have an event that causes one of those to go down. The exposure to the company, to the bank, to our balance sheet, to our shareholders, is much more diversified on the small business side. Third, the upside is what happens to small businesses, as they become successful and their projects work, is they turn into cash. So liquidity in these small businesses tends to be very, very high because they realize they're living on the edge in that regard. Larger companies tend to be fully invested. You make much smaller margins on them. They have lots of competitive alternatives that don't include the banks. If I do 10 loans at $100,000, I have $1 million in circulation, highly diversified. If one, two, or three of those hit, I have a very loyal custumer over a long period of time. I would much rather do those deals. That is why we at Huntington are the largest small business lender in the Midwest, and have been for many years, because we believe the small business company and the small business owner are the same. So if you underwrite the owner, you've underwritten the company.[9]

That is in fact what happened when I wanted to borrow money to buy a building. The loan process was simple and progressed fairly quickly. Having said that, I know that there are those out there shaking their heads because they have not had a good experience with traditional lenders. Indeed, the NSBA Access to Capital Survey says that 60 percent of the small businesses use a large bank, followed by a community bank, and then credit unions. However, large banks come in third place for a positive rating.[10]

What should you look for in a traditional lender? Dunlap has an answer:

> Traditional lenders have extraordinary expectations that aren't always sensitized to small business. So you've got to be careful. A 'bad Friday' is when someone doesn't let you extend on your line, you can't exercise a buy opportunity, and/or make payroll, and you're not in existence anymore. You have to be very careful to make sure that you have patient and friendly capital, a bank that understands small business. Sometimes small businesses can't make that connection, and that's why most small businesses go to family resources or other non-traditional resources, which are highly acceptable in some cases.[11]

The top three funding sources

According to the NSBA Access to Capital Survey, the top three types of financing are revolving lines of credit from a bank, credit cards (which every person I spoke with says you should avoid), and bank loans. After that, individuals get creative. The study confirms that one of the types of financing that many individuals use (almost 20 percent) is a private loan from family or friends.[12] For decades it seemed to be an unwritten rule: don't borrow money from family or friends. But, in truth, this is how many small businesses have gotten their start during the years. And, as credit has gotten tighter, family and friends are stepping up even more.

When my sister, Vicki Phaneuf, and her husband, Charles, decided to buy their business, it was a typical story. No one wanted to lend them money. He was a consultant at the time and she had a part-time job. The business they wanted to buy was a "sleeper." It was a small party-rental company in North Carolina called Chair and Equipment Rental, now CE Rental. But it had the potential to grow given the right owners. I am not sure how the conversation got started, but it became obvious that the only way they could afford to buy the business was if they had help. I asked my accountant to look at the books. I knew that my sister was a good business person. Her husband worked in the automotive industry for years and had an MBA. They were a great bet, but financial institutions were not in the mood to bet. In the end, my business and the family made them a loan. We had a contract, an interest rate that was good for them, and more than I could have gotten for a CD or from a money market account. It's that concept that Jim Dunlap talked about—it has to be mutually beneficial. In our case, it was!

Today, CE Rental in Raleigh, North Carolina, serves the entire Triangle Area and beyond, and it has grown into a gem of a business worth about 50 times the original price. The loan was repaid long before the note was due. Now banks are clamoring to lend them money. My sister noted that her bank came to "hand deliver a check for a new truck that we needed." On the financial front, things have definitely changed for this small company in a big way.

Years ago, there were not the online resources that exist today for those who want to lend money to a family member. Loans were made quietly and sometimes without a lot of safeguards in place. Today, there is a proliferation of lending

Websites that can provide guidance and help. For a small fee, these sites will set up formal loans, complete with interest and repayment terms. In the beginning, these sites were for lending to family and friends; now they extend to a variety of different investors.

Alternative lending

Marilyn D. Landis, President of Basic Business Concepts, Inc., knows a lot about alternative lending. That's because, as a commercial lender, she was exposed to hundreds of entrepreneurs who were talented at developing their product or service, but typically lacked the financial expertise needed to run a company. She also worked for three of the largest SBA lenders in the country. During her career, she has secured financing for income properties, construction projects, manufacturers, restaurants, and hotels, handling loan amounts from micro-loans to $22 million in funding.

When Landis launched her business back in 2001, she believed that smart entrepreneurs could position themselves to do more than just survive; they could thrive if they had the needed access to affordable CFO-level skills that were customized to each business. Essentially, her company acts as the CFO in the corporate executive suite (C-suite) for small businesses. She says that businesses have a host of options when it comes to financing. The trick is to know where you fit. On one end of the spectrum, there are micro-loans from economic development agencies. If you fit their model and they understand your business, they can make you small loans, for example $5,000, $20,000, or $50,000, to buy that piece of equipment you need. On the other end are high net-worth individuals who are direct lenders or investors. Landis cites an electrical contractor who made millions in his business, and then set up a pool of money to lend to other electrical contractors. These high-net individuals are very savvy about a particular type of business and want to lend in that market niche. Be aware that some of these private lenders, in addition to providing funding, are very hands-on with business plan support.

Landis says that individuals try to put the alternate lending market into one bucket, but it is very diverse. One thing to note: no matter what type of funding you seek in the alternative market, you have to do your homework to find reputable sources because this is an unregulated part of the financial market. Landis says you should find out what others' experiences have been with these lenders because "you might discover that your angel is really a devil."[13]

Recognizing the need for reliable funding sources, many business organizations are working to try and help businesses and lenders find each other. The National Small Business Association (NSBA) did just that when it partnered with an alternative financing company called On Deck Capital. On Deck has delivered over $400 million nationwide to more than 700 different industries into what they call a "critically underserved market."[14] The loans range from between $5,000 to $150,000 for existing small businesses, such as restaurants, retailers, and other small service providers. The loans are designed for short-term uses, such as purchasing equipment or inventory, facility upgrades, adding employees, or general working capital. To qualify you must:

- Be in business at least one year.

- Have at least $100,000 in revenue.

- Have at least $3,000 in average monthly bank balance.

One of the things borrowers will find with this alternative lending source and others is that the borrowing process is fast, simple, and transparent. Unlike the reams of paper you need to submit with some other types of loans, the application process is a one-page online form and takes about 10 minutes to complete. Loans are approved based on three months of bank processing, or three months of merchant processing. Here's the part that really makes you take notice: decisions can be delivered in as fast as one business day, and funding in as fast as two business days.

How can alternative lending sources approve businesses and react so quickly when some traditional ones cannot? On Deck Capital uses technology that seamlessly aggregates digital information—such as cash flow, merchant processing information, and social data—to evaluate the true health of a business. And here is the good news: On Deck Capital also has a help desk for business financial questions.

Of course, you can expect to pay more for money from these sources, but that does not seem to bother some small companies. They believe that speed and ease are the main priorities in looking for funding. Some experts also believe that paying a higher interest rate is not necessarily bad. Business owners who pay more may be better prepared when the artificially low rate cap comes off interest rates. Landis says, "Small businesses that are being pushed out of the banks are going to this alternative lending market, and they are going in with better discipline, better financials, better understanding. Because the money is expensive, they are already paying market risk-based interest rates. They're being more careful with it. They're actually going to be better off in the future."[15]

In addition to these types of lenders, there are also a variety of peer-to-peer lending Websites. Landis has a number of examples of businesses that have been successful getting the money they need from these sites. One such Website is Bolstr. It uses a Web-based marketplace to help individuals invest in and support local neighborhood businesses. It is a true investment, in that the investor has the right to a percentage of the revenue for a period of time. The idea is that the investor will use local word of mouth because he or she will want to see the business succeed and earn a bigger profit share. Generally, the small business is reaching out to raise a little money from a lot of people in their network. This could be a retail store, a restaurant, or a drycleaners, for example. It's a way to support local businesses.

Of course, there are countless other Websites like Kickstarter that facilitate fund-raisers for early stage companies. There's even a company called Receivables Exchange, which Landis favors. It's like the eBay for selling your accounts receivable. It's an online marketplace where you can gain access to working capital by auctioning invoices. There is an area for small- and medium-sized businesses, and one for public and large corporations. Landis says it is the coolest thing in the world and she provides this example of how it works:

Say I'm a CFO sitting at my desk and everything is fine with my cash flow, and suddenly my salesman is bringing this big contract. I've got to get running on this and I need the cash today. I've got this receivable that's coming due in 30 days. I'm going to sell it. So I post it on the Internet, and within four minutes I could have it sold. I get the best rate and term. Several people will bid on it. Now I've got that money and it allows me to buy the raw materials for the new contract. We're off and running.[16]

Landis admittedly prefers alternative lending to traditional sources for a variety of reasons, but she offers a few words of warning, "I work with my clients and tell them it is like credit cards. If you live on your credit cards, it's going to kill you. You have got to know when to get in and when to get out. You have to have a strategy."[17]

Here, Marilyn Landis and Jim Dunlap agree. You need to know when to disconnect from a funding source. But Dunlap goes further:

Make sure you get capital from the right source, for the right stage of your company. Early on, you may need online sources for micro-loans. I would tell you they are compelling and have a good business plan. But I believe that later on you need to evolve and get where you're more traditionally supported so you can have a more robust relationship. Alternative sources don't offer the things that normal financial institutions do, such as business plan analysis, advocacy of underwriting, reference checking on new businesses that you may want to work with, even connecting customers with customers. We have over a million business customers in the Midwest, so there's a likelihood somebody is thinking about or doing something that you're currently doing. What if we put the two of you together? You each benefit and learn from each other. If we can't be the underwriter, we can still be the advice-giver and we don't charge yet—shame on us, for the advice we give.[18]

With the recently-passed Jumpstart Our Business Startups Act (JOBS) legislation, Congress created a "crowdfunding" exception to securities registration requirements. That allows businesses to raise up to $1 million in any 12-month period over the Internet from individual investors. Usually it's $10,000 or less per investor. That's a little good news for small business because the battle to secure funding is constant. It does not end because your businesses' needs never end. There is a proliferation of Websites ready to help you use this new funding tool.

How you manage money and your credit is one of the most critical aspects of business. In one final piece of advice, Landis says to check out the Risk Management Association (RMA) averages. You can get a subscription for service or find it at a business library. This gives you important information by the North American Industry Classification System (NAICS) code on points such as: average profit margins, what percentage the employer gets paid, what the employees get paid, how many days they have to get paid on their receivables, payables, leverage ratios, and much more. It is historic information divided by company size and by asset size. Knowing how you stack up is critical, according to Landis, who says, "So what you have to do is take that responsibility on yourself. The alternative market won't discipline you. Banks won't discipline you. You have to discipline yourself. Good financials, good control of borrowing; don't over-borrow, don't over-leverage."[19]

TIPS TO GET YOU THINKING BIG

- There are a number of different options for accessing capital, and you should understand your needs at a specific point in time to find the best source.

- Do your homework. Be prepared to provide all the documentation needed.

- Check out your lender. What have others experienced when working with them? In the age of the Internet, go digging to find independent comments.

- If you use alternative lending, get in and get out quickly.

- Remember that traditional lenders provide much more than just capital.

- If many lenders say no, there is a reason; you should listen.

5

HIRE THE RIGHT PEOPLE AT THE RIGHT TIME

Long hours. Nonexistent weekends. No personal time. New business owners expect that they will spend most of their waking hours working, and they certainly can if they want to. Every entrepreneur knows that it takes a lot of sacrifice to build a business, especially if you are going after big customers that have big needs. Call us crazy, but we thrive on getting the work done—no matter how many hours we have to spend. There are, however, some business consultants and owners that I think are bordering on delusional. I don't understand those who say you can work a four-hour work week. I think not. I know a few who believe you should only answer your e-mails or pick up voice mails once a day so you can be more productive. And others say you don't need to have your cell phone on 24/7. Just try explaining to your customer why you didn't respond to a call for help when they had an issue at 9:00 p.m. on a Friday night. Believe me; this happens a lot, especially with large customers who consider you to be part of their extended staff. It takes a huge effort to run a great small business. And, when you start to attract larger customers, the effort can become herculean. Ultimately, even I, a steadfast do-it-yourselfer, had to ask, "When is the right time to bring on some help?"

When is the right time to hire?

Many business owners struggle with the decision to hire. They often, procrastinate because they are afraid to make a commitment when there is uncertainty about new legislation, taxes, and the like. Hiring is, indeed, an art in itself. There are lots of consultants and tools to help. There are personality tests like Myers-Briggs, DiSC Assessments—even Dr. Phil has one. These tests can help reveal aspects of a person's character or psychological make-up. I have used some of these tools and even a consultant or two. But ultimately it's about *you* knowing the right time to hire, and then finding the right people. So how do you do that? Let's start with when to hire. I think there are milestones, conditions, and events that trigger this decision.

The most obvious one is that you simply cannot get the work done, or the product out the door, in a timely manner. You notice that you don't have the time to communicate with your customers. They are calling you to ask when projects will be done or product delivered. Let's face it, you are underwater. Is it the right time to hire? Will the surge of business continue? Perhaps this is just a seasonal bump in business or due to unexpected conditions, like a storm that causes lots of damage so that construction workers are in demand.

This is when having a little historical perspective can help. If you know that the bump in business is because customers are trying to get year-end projects done, you can plan for it. Too often businesses make knee-jerk decisions; this is the downfall of well-laid plans. You need to be disciplined, or you just might jump and hire someone for all the wrong reasons. Look at your internal operations, and understand the ebbs and flows of the business cycles or seasons. I keep track of my big customers' corporate year-ends. Why? Because many of them have budgets they need to spend down, last minute projects that come up, or work that needs to be completed to meet some plan. These big surges of work can put a strain on a business.

But there may be other reasons you can't get the work done. Perhaps your employees are just not very productive, or don't have the right tools in place to get the job done efficiently. A business owner told me recently that she had to fire an employee for inappropriate conduct. She was very worried because they were going into a busy season, so she took the former employee's work and redistributed it to the remaining workers. She thought this would solve the problem until they could hire a replacement, but a funny thing happened: the work was getting done faster and better than in the past. The employer discovered, much to her dismay, that the former employee was not very productive and that she was spending a lot of time surfing the Internet and shopping online! She did not need to hire another person.

Having the right tools is also critical. At my office, we have five video editing systems, and each one was a stand-alone system. Trying to balance the work was a nightmare. We would load up the video for a project on one system only to discover that something else on the drives was suddenly needed by a customer. That brought work on one project to a standstill. That is not very productive when it happens on a regular basis. The answer was to put the proper tools in place—shared computer video storage. Now, any project can be accessed on any system. There is a lot less waiting around and a lot greater productivity. Giving people the right tools may help save you from having to staff-up for big projects.

Look to fill the gaps

My business recently had a huge surge in the number of projects we were handling. One week I had three crews in four states. Yes, I know that sounds funny, but one crew visited two states. I started to think we needed to add a person. When I asked my staff, I was surprised to find that they didn't want me to hire. Why? They wanted to work more hours during the business spikes and earn more bonus money. That's okay, but the truth is that sometimes you need to really beef up your staff and be proactive. Look at the skill set of your current employees. Is there a gap? If you want to bring in new accounts, or launch new revenue streams, do you have the talent to do that? Remember, new customers require a lot of extra time in the initial phase of doing business, so you will need back-up.

If you add services or new products, you need individuals that have the skills to do the work or the selling. You may not have that capability with your current staff, and it might take too much time to get them trained. When you expand your geographic reach, you need people to cover those areas. Yes, technology has made it easier to work across the miles, but there are many times when you need to be where your customers are to meet tight timelines or provide the responsive service they demand. If your employees are telling you that they are overwhelmed, and you know they are productive and have the right tools, then it's probably time to hire. The biggest reason to hire new talent is to help you have the time to focus on the business, especially if you want to grow, attract big customers, or change direction.

Setting up an employee to succeed or fail

Timing is everything. Bring in a new person too early, and you may not have enough to keep them busy; they get bored and leave. Bring in a new person too late, and they may be overwhelmed by the amount of work that needs to be done. If you have to err on one side or the other, go for too early. Sometimes we set up an employee to fail. That's because we bring him or her in when we are completely overwhelmed. The people who should be training them have no time. Small business owners are notorious for thinking employees will magically get it and become assimilated into their organization. They might receive basic orientation—how to use e-mail, the phone system, where to find things, etc., but they are not getting what they really need: proper and strategic onboarding. That's much different than a simple orientation.

Onboarding can create employee superstars

When you run a small business, so much knowledge of your company (such as its mission, how it works) is in your head, not on paper. I am not saying that is good, but it is usually the case. You need to write all that information down and share it if you want employees to be superstars. When it comes to the business, they need to know:

◻ Company history.

◻ Mission—the task that it is every employee's duty to carry out.

◻ Values—what's important, and what do you believe in?

◻ Vision—where is the company going?

◻ How do customers view the company, products and services? Who are your big customers?

◻ What are some of the biggest opportunities and challenges?

Then there are the cultural aspects of the business which are just as important, if not more important, than all the business information. I say that because small companies are often tightly knit. You can't go and hide somewhere or avoid your fellow workers. When it comes to the company culture, employees need to know:

- How do you make decisions? Is this a collaborative effort? Is the business owner the sole decision-maker?

- What is the personality of the company? Usually, in a small company, it mirrors the owner's personality.

- Are there some rules that everyone knows but are not written?

The right person for a small business

So now that you have determined that you need to hire and you have thought about the process of onboarding, is there a right person for your organization? Yes! And here's a really important thing to know: the right person for a small business looks very different than the right person for a big business. Many job-seekers are interested in companies with recognizable names or prestigious addresses. They are really excited about titles; the longer and more impressive sounding, the better. They need defined job descriptions, and they want the perks that come with a larger organization. These are individuals that probably won't do well in a smaller company where it will be all hands on deck. In a small company, employees may walk into something new and different every day. They need to be comfortable with uncertainty, and actually get a rush out of the unexpected things that may happen every day.

I made a huge mistake with an individual that I thought would be the right person for our company. She worked at a large retailer in the marketing department. In her position, she was responsible for a variety of different types of communications, including video. She decided that she wanted to make a move to a smaller company where she thought she would be a better fit. In fact, she sold me on how excited she was to work in a setting where she could be hands-on with projects. It did not take long for me and the rest of the staff to figure out that the fit was miserable. She believed she had the skills to do the job and spoke articulately about handling the job requirements.

The problem was that she did not realize how little she actually did at her former job. There were lots of people to support her, and much of the real work was being done by those around her. She was directing the work, not doing it. When she tried to do the work for us, it did not meet our standards. It all came to a head when a big client called and told me never to send her out again because she simply did not know what she was doing. I tried to coach her, but she was not the right person. She was a better fit for a big company. When you do not find the right people, you are putting yourself at risk. Clients who know your company come to expect a certain type of person as an employee. When someone does not meet their expectations, they start to question how good you really are and if they should be working with you.

You might wonder, "How long do you wait before terminating someone that just does not measure up?" I have a 90-day probation period. Some companies have less, some more. I can usually tell within the first 90 days if someone has the potential to be a good fit, but even I have been fooled. Some people are on their best behavior until they are off probation, and then you see a very different individual than the one you hired. One thing I can tell you, the really great employees shine and you know it immediately. The really terrible ones are also easy to spot. It is those that fall in the middle that test your ability as a manager. Pay close attention to these individuals.

Think about new ways to recruit

How do you find the right person? Traditional methods of recruitment, such as placing ads and using temporary workers work for some, but may not be the best options. I've tried wading through piles of resumes and conducting marathon interviews. It can be time-consuming and often fruitless. I tried a staffing company; they posted the job and did the initial interviews, but did not turn up great prospects. In fairness, maybe we did not communicate our needs and wants effectively to them. Or maybe we just didn't use the right search firm. You need to look for the right people in the right places.

Some of my best hires have come from extremely targeted efforts. The last time I needed a project manager, I did not place ads. I wrote one, but then used my connections on LinkedIn to spread the word. I was very clear with my contacts. I asked them to only send me individuals that met the requirements *and* that they believed would be a good fit with our company's culture. Because these people knew us or had worked with us, they got it. The response was amazing. I interviewed at least three individuals that could do the job and would fit in with our culture. It was just a matter of a few weeks and we made an offer. Think about it: no expense, no ads, no wading through countless resumes of people who did not even meet the basic requirements. Now, it doesn't always work, but when it does, it makes hiring easy. For this kind of personal and targeted effort to work, you have to be extremely well-networked with your online community and within the professional circles that are key to your industry. Otherwise, you will not get a great response when you reach out for help.

Don't focus on specific skills: think bigger

Let's say you get excellent referrals. Now how do you make sure the individual is the right person for a position? I find that employers always seem to have a list of skills that are needed for the job, and fairly well-defined experience in terms of years or capabilities. I have found a better way. I don't just look for specific skills because I think you can teach skills. I believe you can't teach the kinds of things that really make an individual successful, and that can help your business as you try to connect with and win big business. Ultimately, you won't know if you have the right person until they start working for you. But here are a few things to consider when looking at a candidate.

◻ Creativity: Does the individual look at the job with fresh eyes? Can they see ways to influence the process, the product, the others around them? Do you think they have the ability to inspire others to think in new and different ways?

◻ Motivation: Does the individual really love what they are doing? I often ask this question: "If you weren't doing this, what would you love to do most?" If they have something they want to do more than the job you are offering, then walk away. Are they motivated to keep learning? Do they take the initiative to stay up to date on things like software, equipment that you might need, and trends in the business? My staff has turned thumbs down on candidates because they did not believe that they would be a good fit, work as hard as the rest of the team, or have the right attitude about serving our big customers.

◻ Problem-solving: Some individuals want you to tell them what to do and how to do it. Business moves too fast to hold someone's hand or direct every move, even at entry-level jobs. We need employees who can solve problems and think on their own. Of course, this means you will have to accept the fact that they might not solve it the way you do. But as long as the job gets done with great results, that is what is important. This is especially critical to your business when there are few hands on deck with a lot to accomplish.

◻ Communication: The ability to communicate is also high on my list. We have washed out a number of skilled applicants because they simply could not carry on a conversation. Maybe this is the result of too much Tweeting and texting. Communication is a broad area; we stress verbal, non-verbal, writing, phone-skills, video conferencing, and much more. When you work with larger customers, who may or may not be geographically close, you need to be an expert at communication.

◻ Attitude: While the right skill-set is important, the right attitude—a willingness to work hard and learn—is the most important trait I look for in a new employee. I look for individuals who are "all in." They will do whatever it takes to get the job and keep it. I've seen job seekers boldly walk into an interview with their list of wants. They want a regular schedule. One individual told me he needed to be home on Tuesdays and Thursdays in time for his wife to go to yoga. I promptly told him I routinely cancel my Pilates session because a customer needs me. They don't want to travel. They want a higher starting pay. I don't always expect to find the perfect fit with a new employee in terms of skill level and experience. I do *want* someone who really wants to work and has a passion for the job.

Get employees involved in hiring decisions

When we interview potential employees, every member of our team has the chance to meet and evaluate them in a one-on-one interview. It's only fair since they will be working and collaborating closely with them. We also do group interviews. This can be intimidating for the job seeker, but you get a chance to see how they relate and their personal style. We do all of this before I talk with the individual. It's a strategy that has some interesting benefits. First, you can get a good read on a person if they are put off by not getting to talk to the boss or decision-maker out of the gate. You get insights from your team because they are looking for different things than you are as the head of the organization. And there is a huge value in including your existing team in decisions that drive the business. They feel and act more like owners when you let them participate in the interview process.

But we don't stop there. We generally ask a candidate to work with us for a day or so, and we pay them. This is a good way to see if they can be a part of the team and use their skills. Anyone can keep up a good front during an interview; it's harder to do that for a day or so. You also see how well they perform under stress.

This system works and I often suggest it to other business owners. One of the few times I did not take my own advice and dispensed with using this process, it was a disaster. I was in one of those knee-jerk reaction modes and we needed to fill a spot for an employee who moved away. One recent graduate looked so promising that I simply hired him. After 60 days, he sauntered into my office and announced he was moving back home—the job was just too hard. I told him that's why they call it work. The experience cost us dearly. We wasted time interviewing him, we wasted money moving him, and we wasted effort on training. The cost of hiring the wrong person is significant, so it's important to get it right for both the employer and the potential employee.

Make room for those with great potential

Sometimes you run across a potential right person for your organization when you aren't even looking. It's tempting to dismiss a job seeker when you don't have an opening, but you might want to think a bit differently. It might be forward-thinking to create a position when you find a talented person. I have done that on a number of occasions. One individual who cold-called our office was so impressive over the phone that I interviewed and hired him, even though we did not have an opening. Today, he is the VP of Production. Employees who get in early and grow with a company can have a very profitable career, and even end up as a shareholder.

The big question is how to afford an individual when you don't have a budgeted position. Here you need to get creative. I have taken temporary pay cuts to bring someone on board. I know other business owners who have used a credit line to fund a position initially. If it is a sales position, you can offer a small base, plus commission, so that the individual is paying for themselves. Remember, you are taking a long-term view of the business when you bring in those with great potential, so you might need to make some short-term adjustments.

The right external team

The concept of hiring the right people at the right time extends to your external team as well. There are a couple of different types of external teams. One is the traditional team you hire; the other is one you access for their expertise, and they look and act like in-house employees but they are not. You are outsourcing that job.

Marilyn Landis believes that small business owners may want to outsource everything except their core competency. She points to encore entrepreneurs. These are generally individuals from the boomer generation who are turning to small-business ownership. Says Landis:

These individuals have great expertise. They don't want to go to work for somebody on their payroll. So you suddenly have this whole raft of very seasoned professionals available who want to be your out-source location for HR, or IT, or ISO 9000, or whatever it happens to be. I have a client in Cleveland, and her entire C-suite, or corporate executive suite, is outsourced. I'm her CFO. She's got her marketing person, she's got her IT, she's got her ISO 9000, and she's got her HR professional. This allows her to bring the highest expertise to the table when she needs it.[1]

This concept is gaining a lot of attention, so much so that the Small Business Administration (SBA) has a whole packet of resources to help these entrepreneurs get started. Of course, there are still the traditional advisors that you use regularly, or on an as-needed basis. These are the individuals that every business needs to advise and guide them throughout the life of the organization. This is not a place to skimp, because you get what you pay for. But to be clear, your needs may change so that team might need to change. In fact, that is almost a given, but I see business owners staying with an attorney or accountant because of misplaced loyalty. Some of your paid professionals may stay with you after the start-up. Others can provide specific short-term expertise to jump start your efforts, but are not needed long-term. Who are these individuals, and how do you find them?

I sought out some of my start-up team. Others found their way to me through business contacts. Some of the team may be obvious, others are not. The attorney who helped me set up the company did such a great job that we were able to use a younger and less expensive attorney during the buyout of my partner. By choosing the right firm with great depth, we are never "over-lawyered" or "under-lawyered." We get the level of service we need, when we need it. A good law firm will help set the foundation of your business for start-up and beyond. And if they do not have the expertise you need, they should get you to the right person to help.

When it comes to an accountant, the right person is not just someone who understands numbers, but someone who really understands business. There is a difference. Many accountants will do the typical work of monthly and quarterly statements, tax returns, and the like. But you need someone that goes way beyond that. You need someone who understands the vision of your business and can help guide you. I sought out someone that specialized in small business. In fact, he was very involved with the statewide and national associations, and advocated for small business. Your accountant should be more than a number-cruncher. An accountant should be a trusted resource.

The right banker should also be a person or organization that does more than take care of your financial needs. He or she should be concerned about helping you make business connections. I'm not just talking about networking. I am talking about helping you connect with big businesses that you want to target. They should also help you connect with other business owners in meaningful ways such as forums, community discussions, and so on. I believe you should look for a bank that is very involved in the community. Not just sponsoring events, although that is great, but also lending their expertise, and their people, to civic and non-profit organizations.

An area where most of us need help is human resources. I was fortunate enough to get some guidance from an HR professional who was a friend of the family. He got me started on the essentials—developing basic policies and procedures, an employee handbook, and basic benefits. Today, it is much more complicated and the world is more litigious. In the past, many business owners thought they needed to have an HR professional on staff; now, there are many more options. You can get help if you are a member of a local or statewide organization. They often pre-qualify resources, and you may get free or discounted services. When looking for HR help, you should know that there are two types of HR professionals. One is an HR administrator. This individual can help you with things like benefits, compensation, and compliance. There are also organizational design consultants. They concentrate on performance management, culture, and coaching. By using these professionals on an as-needed basis, you will be prepared to deal with anything that might arise in this area.

Hiring the right insurance specialist or real estate professional is also critical. Big business knows how to access resources to assess their risk exposures, and they usually have expert insurance and risk management professionals. The reason is obvious: big business is acutely aware of the devastating effect catastrophic losses have on the bottom line. When you are a small company, it is just as important. In fact, your big customers will insist that you have taken steps to manage risk because your "risky behavior" can increase their risk exposure. Often, small business owners rely on anecdotal advice by peers in their industries regarding their insurance needs, instead of engaging an insurance or risk management professional and educating themselves on their own individual insurance program needs.

In the early years, many small businesses treat insurance as optional, rather than a critical expense. They feel they can purchase it down the road, when cash flow improves and their exposure is larger. This is just plain dumb. It makes you and your customers *more* vulnerable to loss in many ways. More and more often, my big customers are asking to see certificates of insurance and understand the depth and capability of my supply chain. I am also conscious that any disruption to my business, even for a day or two, can be disastrous. It means I can't deliver what I have promised, and that affects my customer's ability to deliver. You don't need to know it all. You do need to find an insurance agent or risk management professional you can trust.

Whether the right people are internal or external, you need to hire them at the right time. If you don't, you miss opportunities to connect with and win big business. If you run so lean that customers feel like you are always frantic, you will not inspire confidence. And big customers won't send more business your way or recommend you to others. If you have the right people in place, you become known as the expert and you can take on more business with ease.

TIPS TO GET YOU THINKING BIG

- Don't wait until you are overwhelmed to hire.
- Use non-traditional methods to find the right person.
- The right person for a small business looks very different from the right person for a big business.
- Involve your employees in the hiring process.
- Pay attention to onboarding; it's more than an orientation.
- Think about outsourcing. Will it work for you? What can you outsource?

6

CREATE A GREAT WORK SPACE

Business owners spend a great deal of time thinking about and working on developing their products and services. They often don't stop to consider whether their actual workplace is working for them. The choices are many. You can work at home, share space, or invest in a great space of your own. The old real estate saying is "location, location, location." Yes, location is important, even if you aren't in retail. However, it's not the only consideration. The physical work environment is also critical. You need a great space! You need an office that works for you, a place that gets you noticed.

Over the years, studies by architectural firms and furniture manufacturers have shown that the physical environment has a significant impact on business success. Businesses with great environments generally have higher profits, better employee engagement, and a stronger brand. This is something I learned firsthand. I started my business working out of my home. It was a good move financially because, among other things, it freed up cash to buy equipment. For a while it worked. I had an office and used some space on the lower level for equipment storage. I generally went to the client's location to work, so I didn't need to worry about a meeting space. That was good because it would have been the large, round, oak table (with claw legs) in my dining room—not very professional. It wasn't too long before we outgrew my home office. As we added equipment and started to think about hiring employees, it became obvious we had to look for a facility. The search was on.

We landed a downtown location with plenty of parking for customers, and space to accommodate the equipment. It was not ideal, but it could work, and it did for many years. As we added employees and our clients became more sophisticated, it became clear that we needed something more. We started to look at our physical environment to see if it was helping or hindering our success. We asked some basic questions that I believe every business owner should ask from time to time:

- Has the business experienced change that requires adjustments to the workplace?

- Does the current physical structure work? If not, can it be changed to meet the needs of the work flow?

- Does the furniture support the current technology needs? Do you have computer monitors with

arms to help employees avoid strain? Do you have
wireless capability throughout your facility?

◻ Does the current configuration speed up communication, collaboration, and decision-making?

◻ What are the costs associated with change, such
as new furniture, installation of new equipment,
and downtime?

◻ What is the cost of doing nothing to your space?

Even if the answers to all the questions do not indicate
the need for a change, there is one more important question to ask: does the space project an image that is positive
for the business? Will your customers be impressed by your
workplace? Even if you don't regularly welcome customers or
suppliers in, you still need to think about how the environment affects employees and their ability to get the work done.
In a recent study, "Workplace Wellness Programs in Small
Business: Impacting the Bottom Line," conducted by the
National Small Business Association (NSBA) and Humana,
93 percent of the more than 1,000 small businesses surveyed
said the health of their employees is important to their business's bottom line.[1]

When we looked closely at our space, we realized it was
not great. Our editors sit for long periods of time staring at
a computer. The space also did not reflect our progressive,
technologically advanced company. It was outdated and,
for lack of a better word, frumpy. Our decision was to find
a new location that provided us with a more efficient space
that would be a healthier work environment, and present a
better image to our customers. We also knew that the space

would need to expand and change as the company grew. It took some time, but we purchased a building, and then got some design help to renovate it.

Within a very short time of moving into our beautiful new building with a more open plan, I was amazed at the reaction of both employees and clients. While I can't directly associate new business with the new facility, I can tell you that our big customers took notice. Many of them started coming to our space to work, instead of us having to travel to them. New customers commented on our "cool aluminum walls" and the comfortable chairs. The facility made us look credible, tech-savvy, and impressive. So what should you know about creating a great space? I asked one of my big customers to provide some perspective.

Does your space reflect your brand?

Herman Miller is more than just a furniture manufacturer. It is a 100-year-old-plus company that places great importance on design, the environment, community service, and the health and well-being of its customers and employees. Herman Miller is known for working with large global customers, but they also have much to offer small- and medium-sized businesses that want to stand out from their competition.

Nathan Chandler, vice president of small and medium size business at Herman Miller, says, "I think that small business owners need to be more conscious about whether or not their space reflects their brand. Does it show customers a level of credibility and trustworthiness? Is the space doing the same for employees? Does the space reflect all those things you associate with branding a business? That's particularly important if you have customers visiting."

Chandler says the first priority for the small business owner creating his or her own space is making a smart investment, a quality product that is affordable and looks great:

> With a small business owner, it starts with a really good chair, one that's ergonomically supportive, one that fits your budget, and you go out from there. The table is essentially the new desk. Whether it's an open area or in a private office, it gives you a lot of agility, so you can reconfigure, move things around. The other thing we like to get small businesses to think about is the mixed use of space. If you have an executive office or a private office and you use tables instead of desks, then, if you're not around, your team can meet in there. There is this term that we use called a "cafetorium." It's the combination of the cafeteria or the café area with conference seating or an auditorium. It gives you the hospitality of a community space and a conference space. It's designed for dual purpose.[2]

As you start to attract bigger customers who are used to working in great spaces, you need to ramp up your facilities. But the truth is that a small business has budget constraints, so here are a few things to consider. Look for quality products that have a great warranty. You can go through two or three inexpensive chairs, or buy one really great ergonomic chair that supports your employees and lasts for 12 years. Get some design help. For example, most Herman

Miller dealerships may provide some initial design consulting. Remember that everything in the office, from the furniture, to the artwork, to the colors you choose, can affect both customers and employees. If you want to find out about current trends regarding small- and medium-sized businesses, and much more, visit *www.hermanmiller.com/solutions/small-medium-business*.

Office alternatives

I have spent a lot of time talking about the space, but what if you don't need a separate workplace? I have counseled many business owners to continue to work at home, but improve that space. Today, there are many choices for home offices and resources to help you design one. You don't need to spend a lot of money; you do need to be sure that the workplace works!

Finally, for those who do not need a space all the time, there are more options now than in the past. Building developers and builders have plans for shared space. Some offer your own dedicated area and access to common areas. Others have spaces that you use on a first-come, first-serve basis. You may not always be located in the same place, but maybe that's a good thing that can jump-start new and creative thinking. One thing is certain: things are always changing, so your workplace needs to change as well. I believe creating a great work space will always be a good investment. It will get you noticed by big customers and help to solidify your brand.

TIPS TO GET YOU THINKING BIG

- Businesses with great environments generally have higher profits, better employee engagement, and a stronger brand.

- A great space is a selling tool. It makes you more credible, and encourages customers to visit.

- Employee health and wellness are directly related to the work environment.

- Make buying decisions for the long-term: a quality product will have a better warranty, aesthetics, and functionality.

7

PAY ATTENTION TO SMALL CUSTOMERS—THEY CAN GET BIGGER

Every business owner dreams of landing the big one, the customer or project that catapults their business to the next level. That's why business books on the best-sellers lists have catchy titles, usually about the big score. *Whale Hunting* by Tom Searcy and Barbara Weaver Smith, for example, provides a step-by-step guide for how to land big sales and transform a company. But taking on small projects or customers, the ones your competitors won't bother with, can also reap big benefits and have a large, long-term effect on your business.

For example, one day the phone rang at our office. The caller was a marketing director at a small subsidiary of a global manufacturing company. He was looking for someone to take a PowerPoint presentation and turn it into a short video with narration. Not a big job and not a big budget.

I started to ask questions: "How did he find out about us? Had he done video before?" That's when it got interesting. He explained that the company did have a current supplier; they had worked on a number of projects to date with fairly large budgets. However, this time they were not interested in getting the work. They told him this job was too small for them to be bothered. They only took on big budget, higher-profile projects. It was obvious that the marketing director was frustrated and annoyed. The video was going to be used as part of a presentation to secure new business. It was supposed be that little extra something to help differentiate his company from the competition. The turnaround was tight, and he did not have a lot of time to look for a new supplier. I agreed to meet with him early the next week.

When I arrived, I did not jump right into details of the project; instead, I asked if I could tour the facility. He looked surprised that I wanted to spend the time considering the size of the budget. I explained, "I always like to have more information than I need to do a project." He obliged and took me on an extensive tour of the plant, showroom, and offices. It was very obvious that he was proud of the place and that there could be huge opportunities if they could secure this new business.

When we finally sat down to discuss the project, I did not proceed to show him how we could do what he was asking. Instead, I offered some ideas to make the video more than just a rework of a static PowerPoint presentation. Why not feature the team who would be working on the project, and make it more personal? How about shooting some additional video to entice the potential customer to come and visit? I explained how we could change the scope of the project and still stay within the budget.

It became obvious to my new client that I would devote the time and attention he needed to get this done. After it was complete, he began to send other projects our way—bigger ones. One day, he alerted us that the parent company was looking for a supplier to produce an ongoing communication. He got us on the Request For Proposal list. We responded and showed some examples of our work, including the pieces we created for the subsidiary. Because of our experience, and some coaching from this marketing director, we delivered a great response to the RFP and won the contract.

That first simple $2,500-project opened the door. More than 20 years later, and projects too numerous to mention, we are still working with this customer. The lesson is clear: don't judge a potential opportunity by the size of the budget. Pay attention to what can happen when you help someone and deliver more than they expect.

In a similar situation, CE Rental, a boutique rental company in North Carolina, received a call one day from a woman looking to get a few tables and chairs, along with table settings for a dozen people for a backyard party. Vicki Phaneuf, the owner of the business, said, "I took the time to chat with her about the theme, the set-up, and some other details. When it came down to placing the order, I discovered the customer was outside our free delivery area. I suggested she might want to get what she needed from a closer source."[1] The customer thanked her. A little while later she called back. It seems that the other company was not very interested in her small order. In fact, they were quite dismissive. She placed the order with CE Rental, got great attention and, not long after, called to place a really big order. It seems that this customer was a very successful business person. She had a very large company event coming up and wanted to do business with this small company that treated her so well, even though it was a small order.

There are countless examples like these of companies that simply would not take the time because the project was too small, not high-profile, or just not exciting. There are also examples of start-up companies that no one wanted to service. Great little companies with interesting or niche products can take off. If you pay attention to them while they are small, you might just have a big customer for life.

Are you ignoring people who have the real power?

You also need to pay attention and look carefully at your contacts within the organizations you serve. Many business owners believe that they need to work directly with top management, and ignore those with positions which may not seem influential. That is a big mistake. Here's just one example.

A marketing director at a company we serve had the opportunity to hire a number of individuals to support the field sales department. One individual was a young man with good experience and a lot of ambition. At first, he was managing smaller projects. Our team worked with him and provided the same high level of creativity, quality, and service that we would for much bigger projects.

The young man worked hard, got noticed, and was given more responsibilities; he excelled. The parent company of our client tapped this young man for a professional development program that would put him in line for bigger opportunities. It did not take long. He accepted a position with the parent company at the corporate headquarters. I stayed in touch and was delighted to see how quickly his career was progressing. One day, he called: would I take the time to talk through a potential project with some of his colleagues? He was clear that he was asking for a favor. They already had strong connections to a company that would probably get the job. They just did not want to tip their hand about the budget, or show that they were not as savvy as they should have been about buying this service. As a favor, and not expecting any business from the call, I obliged. Shortly after, I received a Request For Proposal. I was surprised to see that the RFP contained all the things I had coached them to do, such as break the project into phases because the group that does the research may not be as skilled in field production. Needless to say, we bid and won the entire contract. This company has become a major client for our business, and we travel throughout the country to this day to produce pieces for them.

Sometimes the individuals who can help you the most have what appears to be a lower-level position. Stop right there; I know what you are thinking: he or she is just a project manager, administrative assistant, or receptionist. I figured out a long time ago that these are the individuals who are quietly influencing others around them, and their managers rely on them to do lots of research to help them make decisions.

For instance, one day I was scheduled to do a seminar on how to present more effectively at a logistics company. I arrived early, and the receptionist told me that the room was not yet available. Instead of sitting down and ignoring the woman, I engaged her. I asked questions about the company and what she liked about working there. We had a delightful conversation until I was able to go in. Shortly before my presentation started, I noticed that the CEO entered the room and sat in the back. I had not met him prior to that day, but had seen his picture on their Website. I was surprised, since he was not scheduled to attend. The presentation went well and afterward he came up to introduce himself. I asked why he attended and his response was, "Mary at the front desk called me and said, 'You've got to meet this girl.' I wasn't really planning on staying for the whole presentation, but I really enjoyed it." I went on to get a number of additional jobs from this company all because I paid attention to a "small customer."

It's tempting to only target big customers or projects. It's easy to disregard individuals who you believe are not in a position to send business your way. Smaller customers and individuals in middle management positions can be just as important to your business in the long term. That's not to say that big business, or high-level executives, aren't important to our bottom line. Our larger customers have been a tremendous source of referrals. But starting out with smaller customers and projects allows you to really get to know a customer's business and prove yourself.

TIPS TO GET YOU
THINKING BIG

- Look for small companies that have interesting products or services, and are poised for growth. When you build a relationship with a small customer and they grow, you do too.

- Think and act like a student. Try to discover everything you can about a customer or project. Know more than you need to know to do the job.

- Don't blindly do what your customer asks. Offer suggestions or alternatives that improve the final product or help reduce costs.

- The individual with power may not always appear to be influential.

- Think of yourself as an extension of your customer's organization, not just a supplier.

8

RECOGNIZE WHEN TO LOVE CLIENTS AND WHEN TO LEAVE THEM

It's a fact—growing your business with existing clients is much easier than getting new ones. But sometimes you need to take stock of the customer base and see if you still love them, or if it's time to leave them.

When you first start out, you're tempted to take whatever business that comes through the door. Sometimes, it's a customer you don't really want or is one that's not well-suited to your core capabilities. For example, one of my clients wanted us to do car commercials. Yes, those cheesy ones with the owner of the dealership on camera touting a big, once-in-a-lifetime sale. At first, we did these really awful TV spots. Let's face it; even projects you hate pay the bills. But, at least in my case, these small-scale projects were labor and time intensive, and often not very profitable. As I started to study the composition of my client base, I found there were a number of things to consider, including whether I needed to leave or send them away. Here are some points you might want to consider, as well.

First, the work! Is the work something that fits well into your existing workflow, processes, and capabilities of your company? Would it be a stretch to deliver what your customer is asking for, or require a capital investment that you are not prepared to make, like adding inventory? What if it just isn't work that you are ramped up to do? If the work is not part of your core capabilities, it takes longer to accomplish and you get distracted from your base business. I'm not saying that you should just do the "same old, same old," but you also need to think about whether the client can, and will be, good for your business in the long term.

The next thing to consider is the quality of the work that the client is asking you to do. Those cheesy car commercials did not do much for the reputation of my business. If someone was looking at those spots as an example of our work, they did not reflect our ability, or the quality that we could deliver; not to mention that what you attract is often more of what you already have. We would get calls from other car dealers who saw the spots and wanted something similar. This was not the kind of business that I wanted, so I did the unthinkable and made a list of all the clients that we needed to get rid of. I also started to look through our client base to identify those who brought us the kind of work we wanted to do, work that would reflect well on the company and help us attract new big clients. Now I just needed more of them.

Assess the value of what you provide

Every so often, you find a client who you just can't please. You make a recommendation and they fight it, or they simply ignore it. They tell you exactly what they want, you produce it, and they don't like it, but they blame you for the results. They don't provide the information you need to do the job in a timely manner, but they still expect you to deliver on time. It's one thing to run into a snag on a project, or get surprised by something that is out of their control. When that happens, we spring into action and do what a good partner does: we deliver. However, when these types of situations become the norm, then it is time to assess the value of the relationship. The hassle factor may be too great to continue with them.

Another point to consider is the constant pressure from big clients to lower your price, or refusal to pay for things that are outside the scope of a project, or changes that they requested. In the product area, where costs are on a per unit basis, customers use the lure of big volume to try and negotiate a lower price. This is a common occurrence, and while sometimes there is a value to offering a discount, often it puts your company in a difficult position.

Here's just one example. Butterball Farms, Inc. is the largest national dairy supplier of specialty butter and premium butter in the U.S., but it is still a small company. CEO Mark Peters decided to take a calculated risk with a large customer. Here is how he describes the story:

> We worked on a project for about a year with a company where we did the research and development and the flavor profiles. We were very upfront about

the cost of the product all the way through the whole process. We did samples, and we put a lot of money into it over the course of a year. Then, six weeks before product launch, they came and they said, "The pricing isn't going to work. You're going to have to lower your pricing by like 15 cents a pound." That was all of the margin in the product.[1]

Peters went on to say that they simply were not going to lower the price. What ensued was not very pleasant. He told his chief operating officer to call the customer, take him out for lunch, and just say that they had no interest in doing business with their company. As Peters describes it, the reaction of their customer was interesting: "He said, 'Well, don't you even want to negotiate this?' I said no. You know, we found out what kind of character that company had, and I decided the best time to say no to them was before we were reliant on their revenue."[2] Peters said the company took the research and development and produced the product internally. Interestingly enough, they didn't do it very well, and about a year later, they came back through a broker. Butterball ended up making the product after all. He let his customer walk away, but they came back.

This story illustrates a point that needs to be emphasized. When you start to feel like you are getting beat up on price, you need to take a good, hard look. Are you competitive? Will dropping the price seriously impact the financial health of your company? Is the big company using their position to take advantage of you? Will you start to resent the customer, and will that have an impact on the quality of the relationship or on the product? If you answered yes to some or all of these questions, then it is time to rethink your position.

How to leave your clients gracefully

Of course, getting clients to leave is not exactly fun or easy to do. You need to be systematic and thoughtful. You can't send a lot of clients away at once or you face another problem: cash flow. When we decided to take stock of our customers and really focus on the ones we loved, we started by identifying our biggest problem clients. Truthfully, there were not many. That surprised us, but if you think about it, it makes sense. It only takes one child misbehaving in a classroom to change the environment. One difficult client can do the same. It makes your employees anxious, disrupts the work, and just colors everything. We planned our strategy for *when* we would ease clients out and *how* we would communicate with them. For the most part, I think the clients understood. I told them that we were moving in a different direction, and thought that they would be better served by a different type of production company. I had identified a couple of options for companies that could help them and passed along their names. If you are going to send clients away, there is one thing to note: don't just cut off service or product flow; help them make the transition. You never know—there might come a time when you want to welcome them back.

There was one particular client that would not go away. This customer was actually referred to us by another good, long-term client. He sought us out and had completed a number of projects, but he always seemed to be unhappy, and questioned everything we did and every bill we submitted. When I told him about our plan to send them away, he was incredulous. I went on to explain that it did not seem like he trusted our judgment or liked our work. He disagreed and said that was not the case. Evidently, I misread him. That was his way of working and communicating. This client stayed, and now we both understand each other much better. I know to ask more direct questions, and not to take it personally when his face seems to be disapproving. He started to communicate with us a little more and seems to have altered his tone. We both won, because our companies are actually a good fit for each other.

By sending clients away, I had more time to seek out and develop the kind of business that would position the company to move forward with the effort to attract bigger businesses from all over the country. In all honesty, it took a while, but it was well worth the effort. Of course, if I had been a little more choosey at the outset, then I wouldn't have created the situation. So think clearly about the customers you want, and don't be afraid to turn those away who don't meet the profile. Then, work like crazy to get the kind of clients you do want.

When clients want to leave you

Of course, it's important to be prepared for when a client wants to leave *you*. It's bound to happen. No matter how good you are, or how long you have worked with a customer, the day may come when one of them just wants to try someone or something new. This is especially likely to happen if you own a service business or if a good contact leaves a company and is replaced by someone who wants to bring in their own preferred suppliers. So what do you do?

This is the time to be very careful. For a number of years, we produced a year-end communication for a client. When we contacted them one year to start the work, the marketing director told me that they decided to try something different with another company—I was shocked. There was no sign that they were unhappy or even looking to find another supplier. I tried to find out the reason for the switch. I asked a few open-ended questions and just got polite, vague responses, so I did the best I could to respond. I told the client that I completely understood, and that sometimes it's good to try something a little different. I also added that I hoped if they ever needed anything, she would feel comfortable giving us a call.

It took a little while, a whole year, but the client did call us again. It seems that the "something different" they tried did not work out. While I did not probe to find the details, over time they let enough slip through that I knew they did not have a good experience, had paid more, and did not feel that the new supplier lived up to their promises.

Customers we love

While I have spent a lot of time talking about leaving customers, it is also important that we address the customers we love. These folks are easy to spot. They appreciate your efforts, they tell others about you, they send you flowers—really. (I thought it was supposed to be the other way around.) They apologize when they ask you to do something that they know is difficult. They include you in discussions about their plans so you don't get surprised by things that may impact their relationship with you, whether that is a change in their buying habits or their expectations from you as a supplier. These are customers who care about your business and want to be sure that you are successful. They are true partners.

It was not so long ago when the furniture and automotive industries were suffering. As a result, their suppliers felt the impact. At the time, I was doing a lot of work for Herman Miller, but I could see that they were starting to pull back in an effort to cut costs. It was the smart thing to do. One day I was out at their headquarters working with the CEO, Brian Walker. When we finished working, he pulled me aside and said he knew they were not sending as much business our way as in the past. He expressed his concern about my company and wanted to know if we were doing okay. We were. Indeed, we had started to work on diversifying our customer base and were making great progress. The fact that he took the time to care about a small supplier meant everything, not to mention that Herman Miller has referred other clients to us through the years. These are the clients that you love. That is not to say there won't be problems. Client relationships are complicated even under the best circumstances, but when you find clients that you love, protect the relationship. It is invaluable.

Show your appreciation

How do you show your customers that you appreciate the business? Say it every chance you get. Send them an actual thank-you note, not just an e-mail. Try to accommodate them when they have an urgent need, and don't make it sound like you are doing them a big favor. Understand that they have bad days too and need your support. If appropriate, invite them to events that might appeal to them: a concert, the theater, a charity gala. One thing that my company likes to do is to feature customers in our video newsletter. This is a great way to put the focus on them. If you have a blog, you can use that communication to promote them, or causes that are dear to them. You might also feature them in a print ad. Just remember, however, that it is always good to run any of this type of activity by them first, as some of your customers may not want the publicity or attention.

It may sound corny, but CE Rental routinely holds customer appreciation activities. It's not just one event, or a gift to a client; it is a carefully thought out experience that shows customers how important they are to the business. That can be anything from a small intimate cocktail party for those who want to just stop by and visit, to inviting a group of women to a Murder Mystery dinner theater. Owner Vicki Phaneuf says, "The goal is to show how much CE Rental cares about our business clients and to connect them with others. We believe these opportunities are great because they provide a rich and personal experience for the individuals and bring our community closer together."[3] CE Rental also routinely sponsors community events such as a Wine Dinner, where the proceeds go to agencies that help special needs children, or events to benefit the United Arts Council. They also support causes that are near and dear to their customers, such as breast cancer awareness, and the local SPCA. The owners of this rental company spend a lot of time working and playing with the customers they love, and everyone wins.

So think about it. If you are spending your time working with customers who are holding you back from the work you want to do, work that will move you closer to the customers you want to attract, take the difficult action to leave them. And, when the relationship is good for everyone, make sure you show your appreciation. Big thinkers know when it is time to love clients, and when it is time to leave them.

TIPS TO GET YOU THINKING BIG

- ◻ Do you have a profile of your ideal customer? What is the size of the company or the order? What type of industry is your sweet spot?

- ◻ Have you thought about why working with some customers is a joy and working with others is painful?

- ◻ Do you cringe every time a certain customer calls? Do your employees not want to engage with certain customers?

- ◻ How can you go about leaving difficult customers gracefully?

- ◻ What will it take to replace the business that you leave?

❑ Do you show your customers how much you appreciate them in interesting and creative ways?

9

BE AHEAD OF THE PACK, BUT NOT TOO FAR AHEAD

Do you really need to be ahead of the pack to attract big customers? Some believe that is the case, but I would argue that it may not always be true and, in some situations, may hurt your operation. Staying ahead of the pack for a technology company is challenging. In my world, everything changes at breakneck speed. It used to be every two years we would need to redo systems, processes, and equipment; now it seems like things change every two months. Okay, that is an exaggeration, but sometimes it feels like it. You have to stay ahead just to stay even. My first encounter with bumps in technology came when we decided to step out and move into the world of digital non-linear editing. Think of it this way, just as you can cut and paste a Word document, you can also cut and paste video and audio. That might not seem amazing, but back when we purchased our first system, it was. In fact, we were one of the very first in the country to buy an AVID, a very cool editing system. It was the same year that the renowned filmmaker, George Lucas, also bought one to do rough cuts of his movies on site. We were so excited about the technology that, when AVID asked us to be a beta test site, we jumped right in. That was when I learned first-hand about being ahead, but not too far ahead.

As new software updates were released, we were to test them, find the bugs, and report back. Early on, we loaded one new release and it literally turned all our video blue. People looked like smurfs. It took hours to reload the old software and get the video back to normal. Those were hours we simply did not have because of tight deadlines for projects.

We could claim that we were among the first to have the technology, but I am not sure it was worth the headaches, long hours, and the pain of dealing with the disruptions. Today, when new software is released, we wait; we do not jump in to upgrade. We let others work out the bugs and jump in a bit later. It has saved us a lot of grief.

Sometimes it takes more than just one situation to learn the lesson. When DVD technology was first released, I once again listened to our staff get excited about the possibilities. Of course, we had to be the first to be able to compress video and author DVDs. The first DVD systems were well over $100,000. We bought in. Within a year, the cost had dropped dramatically, down by almost a third. The following year it was down again. Here was the problem: if we had made enough money selling the service, it would have been worth it. But at that time, people were still using VHS tapes and did not really care about DVD technology. We tried to educate them, but many felt there was not a compelling reason to adopt this new technology at that time. And big businesses are sometimes afraid of new technology because they believe it is unproven.

The next big revolution was high-definition video. By now, I had learned the lesson well. We let others buy those first new, and very expensive, high-definition cameras and editing systems. We rented what we needed. Sure enough, just as before, some of the formats made it, others did not. By the time all the hoopla passed, we were in good shape. We did not get stuck with an old format or pay too much. We jumped in at just the right time and the right price. Part of what helped us this time was that we went out and asked a few key customers about their interest in using the new high-definition format. We knew that not everyone would be interested, but that there would be a few early adopters of the technology. An early adopter is an individual or company that is very forward-thinking; they tend to try new things before they are the norm.

When we got positive responses about the inclusion of high-definition video into our product offering, we knew we were on the right track. It is a great idea to include customers when making decisions that put you ahead of the pack, but there is one item of caution. Don't just ask if they will use the new product or service; ask if they are willing to pay for it. There is a big difference. They might like to try something new, but when they see the actual cost, there can be a change of heart.

People and ideas make the difference

Being ahead of the pack is not just about technology or equipment, it is also about how you work with employees and serve your customers. Let's start with employees. Today, it's not uncommon that companies let employees modify their work schedules, offer day care onsite at a reduced rate, or supply perks like health club memberships. Some of these things can cost you a lot.

For example, we paid for cell phones for our key employees long before cell phones were popular. We thought we were being progressive, but we should have considered the whole picture. It became a huge cost and, when we had to stop, it was not pretty; our employees considered it to be a take-away. Fortunately, the cost of cell phones has gone down and this is no longer an issue.

There are some things you can do to be ahead of the pack that will get you points. I like to encourage employees to come up with new ways of doing things, such creating a new system for tracking the elements of a project, a new graphic look for a client, or a new revenue stream. To get ideas that keep his organization ahead of the pack, Bob Fish of Biggby Coffee uses an "Idea Box." I know what you are thinking: that is old school, simply a new name for a suggestion box. But it is not just the box; it is how he uses it. As Fish says:

Our operators, anyone in this office, or anybody connected to the company, has access to a larger intranet that we use. Lodged in there is our Idea Box. It is a democratic process for bringing ideas to the table, so anybody can go log an idea. But the real charm of it is that, going forward, anybody else can weigh in on it. Now, there are more ideas than we can process and that's great. But the way we approach the ideas is not in chronological order, it is by order of dialog. So we'll take the idea that has the most traffic on it first.[1]

Fish says they have strategic meetings, tactical meetings, and execution meetings. These meetings include people from various parts of the organization, franchisee, franchisor, and others. They tackle the big ideas by locking themselves in a room, filled with bean bag chairs and other fun stuff, and deconstruct and reconstruct the ideas that will move them ahead.

I believe that customers like to do business with progressive companies. At Cynthia Kay and Company, we have found a few ways to be appropriately ahead of the pack. First, we were progressive in the way that we quoted jobs. Instead of a number, we quote with price ranges; instead of charging for every piece of equipment, we bundle it, and offer everything for one price, no add-ons and no surprises. Our competitors did not do that, so even though our day rate looked more expensive, it was not. When we showed clients how the package price compared with our competitors, we received very positive responses for being progressive.

One of the most progressive things we have done is to eliminate the charge for travel time. Everyone has heard of plumbers who charge from the minute they leave the shop; it's a trip fee. I'm not sure why they get paid for driving to my house. It's not like they are thinking about unstopping my sink or working on a strategy to fix the leaky toilet while driving. Anyway, we were quite progressive in this area, especially if you consider that some of our work takes us across the country. It is a delicate balance to keep your business at the forefront, and you should never just settle in and let others pass you by. This is a lesson that will save you time and money.

TIPS TO GET YOU THINKING BIG

- If you are a small business, weigh the risk of jumping in too quickly.

- If you are going to be an early adopter, you might want to test the water with a few key customers to see if you are on the right track.

- Don't squelch your employee's enthusiasm for new processes, products, or revenue streams. However, be sure there is a good business case to support them. Using a democratic process like the Biggby Coffee model will inspire many ideas.

◻ Being progressive is not just about technology, it is also about how you work with customers and employees.

◻ Check out the competition; not that you should follow them, but they can be a gauge of where you are, and where you may need to go.

10

KNOW WHEN IT'S TIME FOR EMPLOYEES TO GO

In dealing with employees, the conventional wisdom says attract and then retain good talent. Increasingly, books and articles address that issue with advice about how to create a work environment that cares about and nurtures employees. The list of well-known companies that provide sometimes amazing perks is lengthy, everything from a free on-site fitness center or hair salon, to massage therapy and cash bonuses. But is this realistic for a small business? Should you encourage employees to move on from time to time, and bring in individuals with fresh ideas to help you better compete? As you attract bigger businesses, can your employees handle more complex interactions?

Long before it was popular, my dad did a great deal with his dry cleaning business and small burger joint to make the workplace more desirable, and build loyalty with his employees. Without knowing it, he was a pioneer in looking at the whole person, and dealing with both personal and professional issues. In fact, he did things that by today's standards would be considered, well, "crazy." He bailed employees out of trouble; he gave jobs to their siblings and gave advances on paychecks. Dad was so good to his employees that some of them never left.

Take, for example, the case of an employee named "Mark." When he came to work for my dad he was a young man. He started, like most of the others at the Glass Hut, flipping burgers and making chili dogs and fries. Eventually, he became the counter guy. Nothing unusual there, except when all the young people—who started about the same time as Mark—moved on, he stayed. No one could understand why this 40-something year old man was still making burgers.

One day it all became clear: the police arrived asking questions. We later found out that Mark was running a bookie operation out of the store. He was taking bets on everything from football games and horse races to local card games. His job gave him access to lots of people, and it was a great cover.

This is an extreme, but actual, example. While in hindsight it seems comical, I learned an important lesson from this incident: as an employer, I should know when it is time for employees to move on. This is especially critical for small businesses, because employees do not have as much opportunity to move up. As a result, they get comfortable. They often stop trying to excel and they get stale. Through the years, I have seen this happen time and time again.

Perhaps the most obvious case of this in my business was a young woman who began working for the company when we were just a two-person operation. At the time, the company was located on the top floor of a building with an art store below. For a while, "Mary" was a wonderful employee— responsive, attentive, and organized. But as our organization grew, she did not. She became annoyed as we tried to expand our client base and attract bigger and more complex customers. She became more sensitive to any type of constructive criticism.

It all came to a head when we moved from our humble offices to our own beautifully remodeled building. The new offices were modern, had lots of style, and were certainly more reflective of our high-tech business.

From the time we started planning the move, it was obvious that she was not happy. The night before the move, after everyone left, I discovered that she had not made much progress in organizing and packing up our huge library of videotapes. When I could not reach her, I called a few friends and my sister-in-law to help. Late into the evening, we managed to get it done.

The next day, things did not get better. She moved her personal items, but did not stay after hours to help the rest of the team at the new facility. Months later, Mary was still not adjusting to the new facility and our new ways of doing business. She took offense when we instituted a dress policy that required employees to reflect our company brand. She became combative with fellow employees and terse with clients. Why? Perhaps she simply did not like change. Maybe she was more comfortable in a smaller business, dealing with less sophisticated clients. Who knows for sure? What I did know was that it was past time for her to go. I had missed the opportunities to respond to the red flags that appeared over a long period of time. In the end, I fired her.

This is perhaps the most difficult decision that every business owner faces. You want to have a solid staff. You do not want to keep training new employees. You want to show a consistent face to the customer. But if you work with an employee, remove barriers, provide them opportunity and reasonable development, and there still is not enough prog-ress, then you have to let them go. If you don't, the collateral damage to the organization can be great.

In another case, I hired an individual as a producer. During the interview process, he was personable, outgoing, and appeared to have the necessary skills. However, several months into the job, it became clear that "Kevin" was not what he appeared to be. He had managed to put up a good front, but could not sustain it day to day. He was quiet, re-served, and very much a loner—that is a huge problem when you work for a communication company.

I encouraged him to be more outgoing. I went out on lo-cation with him, and modeled how to interact with custom-ers. In the end, he simply did not have the personality to do the job. Several customers told me it was painful trying to have a conversation with him. When I sat down to tell him that I was terminating his employment, I think he was re-lieved. Kevin was not a good fit for our organization.

Since Kevin and Mary left, our organization has progressed and grown. Change is good. The individuals that filled those positions have taken us much further and instituted many new ideas. The business has benefited from their fresh eyes and fresh thinking.

Is it time to go?

In many ways, this is all about alignment. Think about what happens when your spine is out of place. You go to the chiropractor because everything hurts, you can't be productive, and the work you do is not very good. You get an alignment and everything starts working again. The same is true of organizations. When your organization is out of alignment because employees have not grown and changed to fit a new reality, the business can't be efficient or grow. Here are a few questions to ask to help determine if it is time for employees to go:

- Is the employee stuck or ineffective because of something that you have done?
- Have the working conditions changed, and they simply cannot adapt?
- Is the employee not being challenged, or not challenging him or herself?
- Are your customers making comments about the lack of service, poor quality of product, and attitude of the individual?
- Is the individual damaging the culture of the organization?

- Is the individual's attitude affecting the morale of your other employees?
- What is the cost of keeping them?
- Can you replace the skill set?

So you made a bad hire. Now what?

Here is one more thing to think about: perhaps the employee was simply a bad hire from the start. If you discover that, even after all of your best efforts, the employee is not right for your company, don't prolong the inevitable. Take a little time, and do a short assessment so that you can have a clear conscience. Ask yourself:

- Were the expectations of the job clear, and did you communicate them?
- Did you provide performance feedback and coaching?
- Did you give the individual all the training and development necessary to be successful? Sometimes people derail themselves. They just don't want to be successful.
- Have you have removed barriers, provided opportunity and reasonable development without seeing any progress?

If you answered yes to only one of these questions, then I think it is time to take bold action quickly. It will save you much heartache later. Yes, you should try to attract and retain good employees, you should take care of employees and

mentor them, and you should help them to grow professionally. But when there is no opportunity for them to move up,
help them move on. When they simply can't perform and are
never going to get there, don't just fire them. Treat them with
respect, talk to them, and gracefully move them out. Besides
the altruistic reason for helping a struggling employee move
on, it's also practical. Yes, it will save paying unemployment
but, perhaps most importantly, it also helps maintain good
morale and loyalty with your remaining employees.

TIPS TO GET YOU THINKING BIG

◻ When employees do not have the opportunity to
   move up, try to help them move on.

◻ Watch for the signs that indicate employees are
   bored or uninterested. Try to understand what is
   happening.

◻ Change is difficult, and some employees simply
   cannot adjust. If you work with an employee and
   there is still little progress, take action.

◻ New employees bring a fresh perspective and new
   ideas.

◻ Always mentor employees and help them grow
   professionally.

11

CHOOSE TO GET BIG OR STAY SMALL

It is a dilemma that plagues every business no matter what the industry, no matter how big the company: do you grow, keep growing, or stay small? How small? This one decision affects every aspect of your business. It's been said that if your business is not growing, it's dying. This, however, is a complete oversimplification of a very complex issue.

Without question, when it comes to growth, there is no one easy answer for businesses. But just Google "grow your business," and you can see that there is a great deal of emphasis on growth and little talk about staying small. There are many strategies for growth, everything from getting deeper penetration with existing customers (one of my favorites), to attracting big customers, to franchising. Your type of business will, in large part, dictate which strategy to pursue.

One terrific example of growth is Biggby Coffee. It has been recognized as one of the top 20 food service franchise concepts in the U.S. by Franchise Business Review. Biggby boasts that it serves the world's best coffee. I know that people's taste in coffee varies, but I have to agree. The first café opened in 1995, the second two years later. The franchise took off in 1999, and since then it has enjoyed a growth rate that has ranged from 15–50 percent every year. Today, there are more than 165 stores in seven states. The growth was no accident. CEO and co-founder Bob Fish said he knew from the very start that he wanted to grow. Some of this can be chalked up to personality. Fish, like most entrepreneurs, gets bored easily. He knew that he was much more than a manager and he did not want to do the same thing over and over again. That meant that, unlike his mom-and-pop competitors, he needed to build more than a one-operation shop. Fish is a dreamer, and when he dreams, he dreams *big*. Says Fish:

> One day, we're going to be bigger than Starbucks. Our vision is to be the largest U.S. franchise specialty coffee shop in America. Now that might seem ludicrous because, you know, the first time I had that particular vision was when we had five stores. And so now we have more than 165, and they have 10,000 stores. It seems like a ludicrous statement, but it doesn't matter to me. When I first made the statement, I wasn't ranked. Now I'm fourth in the nation. Do I think I'll be third? Yes. Do I think I'll be second some day? Yes. Do I think I could be first in the U.S.? Yeah, I do![1]

Of course, getting there takes hard work, but entrepreneurs know that you have to have a destination or you won't get there. In the case of Biggby Coffee, one of the things that moved them ahead quickly was a simple but important thing that most entrepreneurs forget to do: write it down! As Fish says:

I didn't always know all that I know today about how to grow. Things emerged over time. I believe that if you want to grow, you have to learn how to write things down and codify them. One of the first things that I developed was an operating philosophy. And the operating philosophy revolved around the idea that every operation has a set of standards that they live by, including standardized recipes and procedures. But there's an element in an original location that is different, and that's usually brought on by the owner themselves. And so, what is it that can be codified in an operating philosophy that would allow that to carry on? For us, it was a simple four-point system we call PERC.[2]

PERC stands for: *p*erception by customers that we respect their time and move them as quickly as possible; *e*very customer leaves the store in a better mood than when the customer arrived; *r*ecognize each customer as an individual; and *c*onsistently produce a high quality beverage.

Most people believe that when companies are born, they somehow automatically have core values, vision, and a mission. Fish believes it is an evolution, and that's another reason why you need to write things down. If all the knowledge rests in the head of the owner, then you just can't grow. Someone else has to know it, understand it, and act on it. To be sure that there was common ground, Biggby developed its seven core values, and they have not changed to this day:

1. Simplicity through systems: having a system makes it teachable.

2. Be top-line driven because revenue solves all problems; to focus on the top line is to focus on the customer. After all, there is no bottom line without a top line.

3. Energy, excitement, and enthusiasm: it's how you move forward in the world.

4. Always have faith, confidence, and courage. You have to believe in yourself, or no one else will.

5. Maintain long-term sustainability through profitability; profitability is a choice, and it's the only choice that ensures sustainability.

6. Engage with the community; giving is getting.

7. Be defined by your dedication, dependability, and desire—an insatiable hunger to improve.

Those who become franchisees understand the importance of being on the same page. As Fish puts it:

They're going to execute our model. If we don't have the same or similar core values, we'll break up. It'll be a marriage that doesn't work. I was up to four

CHOOSE TO GET BIG OR STAY SMALL

147

units before I said, uh oh. So we're expanding, but where? That's when vision and mission were unleashed. Mission for us is simple. It's something that I can follow every day, and it's something that somebody who started yesterday can follow every day. Our mission in life is simply to create one new Biggby Coffee fanatic per day, per store, who will actively promote us to others.[3]

The last thing that was codified for Biggby was really the premise of the first store. Biggby wanted to serve coffee in a fun and unintimidating manner. While vision, mission, and core values are internal, Fish says that the company culture is the hardest thing to define because it's external. These values have to resonate with the people who *don't know you* and people who *do know you*. That includes potential customers, existing customers, employees, and even your suppliers. According to Fish, "If any of them smell any disingenuousness, it is over. So it has to be real. Cultural values were the last thing to be birthed in our system. They are be happy, have fun, make friends, love people, and drink great coffee."[4] No wonder they are growing.

No matter what type of business you have, growth can be yours if you develop a solid brand and have the infrastructure to support it. There are many definitions of business infrastructure. Essentially, it is the physical and organizational structures needed for the operation of a business. Others say it is all the human resources, processes, and tools you need to ensure that you can manage your growth and be profitable. I like to keep it simple:

- What do you need to do?
- Who in your organization is going to do it?
- How can they get the work done?
- What tools do they need?
- Is there a model, or some formula, so that you can have repeatable success?
- What happens if something goes wrong? Or if you have an unexpected growth spurt?

Without infrastructure, you just can't grow or, for that matter, even run a really efficient small business that wants to stay small. The infrastructure needs to be appropriate for the rate of growth that you are trying to achieve. Then you have to link all of these things together so you can consistently deliver a good product or service, and keep your customers happy. When you do that, you increase sales. That usually means you need to hire more people, maybe get bigger offices or warehouses or, like Bob Fish, turn the business into a franchising opportunity. With a franchise, the franchiser develops the concept, the brand, and all the execution modules. Fish says that the rate of growth can be limitless, and it is the result of an intense focus on the business:

> There has to be a high degree of focus on the things that are going to truly carry you forward. There are a lot of choices that every business owner has to make, but the focus should be on what is going to be the most productive. I ask myself, "What is the one thing

that I can do that will move my business forward in this next year?" I think most people get caught up in minutia that doesn't matter.[5]

Three things to consider if you want to grow

If you want to grow, there are a few things you should consider. First, you simply can't do everything. And you certainly can't do what you did when you were a much smaller organization. There isn't enough time, and you get pulled in so many different directions. You will need to do that thing that so many business owners hate—delegate. Just because you *can* do something does not mean that you *should* do it. Second, some business owners, like Fish, actually give their schedule to someone else to manage so that their time is strictly controlled. Why? Because it's easier for someone else to say there is no room on your schedule to meet or attend a function. When your schedule is not overloaded, you have the time to do the important work that will grow your company or seek out new, big customers. You have the time to focus. Finally, while you may not compromise when it comes to the quality of the product, you might need to make other compromises if you want to grow. You might have to narrow your product line, outsource some of the activities, or simply not do some things.

We have all seen those stories about the fastest growing companies. They are on the covers of magazines one year and gone the next. Why? Perhaps it was a miscalculation or some unforeseeable event. But maybe something else is occurring; something that Bob Fish says is all too common:

If your ego drives your need to expand, you might lose. If there are strong economic reasons, that is our preferred method of growth. The standard question for us is, "How many states are you in?" And I never liked that question because it's like, "How big are your muscles?" Is that the measuring stick; how many states I am in in terms of how successful I am? If I had one thousand units and they were all in Michigan, I'd be the happiest guy on earth. But if I had a hundred units and I was all over the United States, I'd be a failure because it's only two units per state. So the farther I push out, the riskier it is, in terms of the success rate. I can open another store in Michigan tomorrow and it will be successful on the first day that it opens because I am opening it within our sphere of influence. And from a distribution and a marketing perspective, it is the most effective store for me to open. So again, it is this idea of focus. We do have stores that are farther out. We have some in South Carolina; we have some in Texas; but in terms of them benefiting from the visibility of the brand, it's very low. They have a guaranteed system, but they don't have that brand exposure. My ego could drive me to open in at least 20 other states, and it would be pretty easy for me to sell those franchises. But I won't allow that to happen. I won't allow people to open too far out of our geographic hub yet, unless they are convinced and they have the capacity to survive the building of the brand in their particular area.[6]

In fact, Biggby Coffee recently announced it is looking to open more than 130 shops in the Metro Detroit area. That would be about one store for every 30,000 people—that's the focus Fish was describing. By concentrating on this one large market, Biggby will see if it can dominate a larger market, and be closer to the goal of becoming a national coffee chain.

A different choice

While Biggby Coffee is focused on growth and making every single store profitable, I know of many small businesses that make a very different choice. They choose to stay small. They are interested in solid, steady, and measured growth, but it's not what drives them. They want to keep greater control of the product. They do not want to build lots of infrastructure, or have multiple facilities or operations to manage. They don't want to constantly have to seek out new customers who require them to make more capital investments and hire many more people. In effect, these small business owners don't want to build a machine that needs to be fed. My company is that type of company. But just because you choose to stay small, does not mean that you can't do big business.

From the start, I made a conscious effort to think about how big I wanted to grow my company. What would be my ideal size? Was it 15 employees, more than 20, or less than 50? Would staying small let me be choosier about customers? Could it give me more freedom? Could I actually be more profitable doing less work? Many of the small businesses in the U.S. today are one- or two-person shops. I started out that way and now have grown to eight employees. I could have grown faster, but it would dramatically change the business and the way I run it.

Choosing to stay small has an impact on every aspect of the business, from the relationships you have with employees and customers, to the control you have over the product—not to mention the amount of money you need to generate in order to keep the business healthy and moving forward.

Let's start with control. I admit I am a bit of a control freak; I like to have my hands in all different aspects of the business. When I first started, I did it all. I was selling, writing, going on location to do the interviews, and even editing. I knew, though, that I could not continue to do that. However, I still wanted to have the personal contact with each client. I wanted to be able to design, create, and influence the projects. It's a simple fact that the bigger you get, the more removed you become from the actual work.

When I started to hire employees, I did not need to "wear all the hats," I was able to offload some of the tasks. Generally, they were the things that were predictable and did not require my high level of expertise. I still got to do the fun parts of the work and, with only a few employees, I did not end up spending all of my time managing people. I had the time to really focus on our customers. I could spend the time I needed to turn out the best product, instead of feeling under pressure to just get it done. I can visit a customer site, do the research I need, and get to know the people and the companies with which we work.

As we have added more employees, I have tried to hire people who are not only very skilled and talented, but also people who are self-directed. By staying small, I can interact with every person, every day. I don't need to have a gatekeeper that manages my schedule—I control it. We don't have voice mail. I know that sounds really old-fashioned, but it is not; it keeps every interaction personal. I also like the environment of a small company as everyone knows everyone else. They like each other and spend time together outside of work. Every employee also knows about every current project. If a customer calls, they can answer questions, and help them solve issues.

Some bigger companies achieve that small company environment by limiting the size of their facilities. Take, for example, a company that has a group of engineers working on a project. As new projects come in and they need to add people, they don't expand that location; rather, they open a new one. This helps people stay connected and be more engaged. For us, the bottom line is that staying small helps us to provide very personalized service.

Another benefit is that we don't have to load up our schedules to keep everyone busy. I know companies that take on projects that they don't want because they are not at capacity. Let's face it, you don't want people sitting around or equipment idle. You can be really efficient—lean and mean—when you have a core set of capabilities and stick to doing only that work. If you choose to stay small, you probably don't need a big sales force or lots of leads to fill up the pipeline. You need a few really good, big, solid customers that like your work.

One other point: as a small company we can react quickly to changes. I can add new products if we need them. I can move people's schedules around to meet a customer need. We are not paralyzed waiting for a decision on something. We just do it.

Whether you choose to get big or stay small, there are some things that are a given. You still have to deliver a quality product every time. You have to stay relevant; you have to keep it fresh, and you have to be profitable. Staying small doesn't mean your bottom line is small. Stay small? Get bigger? You choose—but don't just let it happen; instead, make it a thoughtful choice.

TIPS TO GET YOU THINKING BIG

- What are the advantages to your business if you choose to stay small? What are the disadvantages?

- What are the advantages to your business if you choose to grow? What are the disadvantages?

- Is there anything preventing you from growing the business? If so, how can you move these things out of the way?

- Do you have the right business infrastructure to support the business, whether it is big or small?

- If you stay small, or smaller, how can you maximize your profitability?

◻ If you decide to grow quickly, do you have a plan? How can you do it responsibly so that you do not jeopardize your business, or the quality of the product or service?

12

THE BIG BUSINESS BUYER'S
PERSPECTIVE

For a number of years, my company has been working with Siemens Corporation and other large global firms. The relationships have been good. They have helped me to understand the buying process in more detail, and connected me with other large companies. So I reached out to try and get a clear picture of the current big business perspective on working with small companies.

According to Carl Oberland, vice president of supply chain management, North America Region for Siemens Corporation, there is a difference between the service-focused small business and the manufacturing products-focused business:

If you're in a pure services side of the business, to my way of thinking, it's a bit easier to do business with big companies. That's because the smaller service company is largely selling people's individual competencies, capabilities, and the ability to match up culturally to the big company client. In addition, the flexibility and the ability to tailor the offering to what the client needs exactly may be easier on the small business side than it is in a big player's house. If the players on a small company team have the right competence, expertise, and experience, then the buying company will not have any reticence to engage.[1]

So that is the service side of working with big business. How about on the manufacturing side or, as Oberland refers to it, "the product solution side"? One of the issues here is the ability of the small business to stay technologically up to date. As Oberland says:

The bigger buying companies, like Siemens for example, typically have a tendency to think that the bigger manufacturing companies have a plan, and that part of their budgets have been allocated toward research and development, as well as property plant and equipment improvement. That is so key! Today the new buzz is toward advanced manufacturing. A smaller player may have a very nice plant set-up that looks very modern. But what we're evaluating is how they're able to stay on top of technological developments over time versus a bigger player. That's what puts them at a little bit of a disadvantage from my point of view.[2]

Ultimately, purchasing organizations will have to evaluate both services-based small businesses and manufacturing-based small businesses as to their business sustainability. This refers to the ability of the business to sustain itself over the longer term. If the small businesses are selling people expertise, then the risk that must be evaluated is whether the business has a fallback plan if key personnel leave the company. If the small business is manufacturing, and has special intellectual property or patents, then the risk to be evaluated is whether access to this technology will continue to be available to the purchasing company, if the small business has a major business interruption or discontinuance.

One area where small manufacturing companies can compete effectively is the production of niche products that big companies need but may not want to manufacture. Take, for example, the case of Butterball Farms, Inc. CEO Mark Peters works with some of the biggest names in fast-food chains, as well as major food producers. Says Peters:

> Our relationship with a major producer of butter is kind of interesting because big companies really struggle with doing niche products. They have their center of the bell curve product lines, but they always want to have a leading edge product. They may want a product that's got a higher margin, or that's not price competitive. The problem is that this is not their core competency. They're not good at making it. So we've sort of defined this market. If it's a product that is under 15 million pounds a year, that's a small market for a large company. But we play really, really well in that space. We can take a product like that,

from test to national scale, and do the whole thing. For the large company, this is a small slice of their business, but it's a high-margin slice. It's never going to be a mainline product for them, but we can deliver this niche-like product and everyone benefits.[3]

So the type of business is one of the pieces of the equation. The second part of the equation is the whole financial picture which comes into play for both service offering companies, and products and solution companies. Most large companies will do a Dun and Bradstreet report, and also ask a potential supplier for a financial statement. This is important because it provides them a good picture of your financial stability—your receivables, inventory, and how your business is faring from a cash flow perspective. This is critical because no customer, large or small, wants to have you come to them partway through a project and say, "I can't go on and finish this unless you loan me some money."

Carl Oberland offers some thoughts on how the buyer looks at this:

> The challenge with small players typically comes into play when companies like ours go to 90-day payment terms. The smaller companies that are offering people services tend to have a little more challenge with their cash flow to be able to handle that. We do have a supplier financing program, which means if we want to pay you in 90 days, we can still arrange for you to get your payment in 15. But you are discounting your receivable a bit. We believe our borrowing rate is much better than the typical firm out there, and

when you discount your receivable from that, you're discounting it at a competitive interest rate that's typically better than what you can get on your own from a financial institution. Many suppliers have signed up for this financing program so that some of the cash flow issues can be overcome.[4]

In this regard, Siemens Corporation has been innovative. Other large corporations have experimented with this type of supplier financing program, and some have benchmarked Siemens. One other point to note: it is not just smaller companies that take advantage of this program; even big firms are utilizing it.

The truth is that small businesses need to understand the position of big business. Oberland describes it this way:

> Think of our responsibility as a triangle. There is the financial side, the quality side, and the delivery side. And the quality and delivery do affect the financial piece. We'll call the financial piece the initial price. It is important that small businesses are able to articulate their ability to satisfy all three corners of that triangle because it isn't always just about price. They need to be able to emphasize their ability to deliver on time, with a quality solution or quality offering.[5]

To broaden this perspective beyond my customer base, I went searching to find another buyer with diverse experience in global purchasing. Christopher Locke has been in the industry for 35 years, with 12 of those years in global purchasing. He is a former senior buyer in the International Procurement Group of DaimlerChrysler. He also worked for

American Axle & Manufacturing in Detroit as senior buyer of indirect and direct procurement. Today, he works as a senior buyer for a world premier solution provider of off-highway, onsite energy and components applications in power propulsion systems. Locke loves the procurement process, so much so that he writes a free blog, *www.thebuyersdesk.com*. There, he provides feedback from behind the buyer's desk and educates those selling to big businesses.

Locke is very much in agreement with the comments from Carl Oberland. He also has some very definite ideas about the advantages and disadvantages of doing business with small and large businesses. Some of this is, as both Locke and Oberland suggest, based on fact and some of it is perception. And, of course, it certainly does not apply 100 percent of the time.

The advantages of working with large companies

First, let's look at the advantages of choosing a big business as a supplier. According to Locke:

> The perception is that a big business is more financially stable and less likely to close their doors. They have more diverse products and services. They can provide products and services nationally, even globally, to all of my facilities. If I just had one facility in one state that would be one thing, but I have facilities all over the world. Smaller companies may not be able to meet my needs for products and services in all of my locations, much less the sales representation.[6]

Locke goes on to say that larger companies have more complex research and development facilities and that often provides a technological advantage that smaller companies simply do not have. Says Locke:

In our mind, larger companies are more organized. Why? Because they have more specialized departments in quality, specifications, research and development, manufacturing, and sales engineering. If you deal with a smaller company, they may not have a good comprehension of what we are looking for because they simply don't have anyone who has the time to read all of the specifications. They just agree to it without fully understanding it. Larger companies are also more likely to be certified to the most updated industry standards.[7]

The disadvantages of working with large companies

If this sounds like Locke is biased towards large companies, he is not. He says larger companies also have many disadvantages. Larger companies have less of a personal relationship with their customers because they have so many clients. They are also less likely to accept the purchase order terms and conditions, including payment terms. Larger companies are slower to respond to e-mails and voice mails. Locke says, "They also have a higher rate of turnover when it comes to sales representation. I'm working closely with someone for three months, then he or she is reassigned, and someone else takes over the account who knows absolutely nothing about my company or what we've been working on."[8]

Locke agrees with others that he is not likely to be dealing with executive management at a large company, and certainly not the CEO. The highest level he might be able to reach is the sales manager, and usually not someone who can make things happen. It is just a fact of life that there is more red tape and bureaucracy in dealing with large companies as suppliers. Locke goes on to say that sometimes larger suppliers simply do not want his business and shares this story:

> I was talking with a few of the buyers at our company, and one told me he received an e-mail that a supplier had mistakenly passed on to him. In it, the supplier said that they didn't even want our business because they felt we were not buying enough from them, or that the profit margin wasn't high enough. So they would rather not work with us at all.[9]

According to Locke, that is rarely the case with a smaller supplier.

The advantages and disadvantages of working with small suppliers

So what are the advantages and disadvantages of working with a smaller supplier? Locke says that smaller suppliers are more willing to ship product or deliver services before receiving payment, or even a purchase order. In urgent cases, smaller companies understand that products are needed as soon as possible so that work can continue at his facility without shutting down the line. I can attest to this point personally. I often have large customers call with last minute requests. I never hesitate to respond because I know that I will get paid. I know that because I have a close, personal relationship with the customer. In 25 years, I have not been disappointed. Another advantage, which almost every person I spoke with mentioned, is that close, personal relationship. Locke says:

> Smaller suppliers will spend more time with me because they have a few key customers. Smaller companies are also more willing to accept purchase order terms and conditions. They have faster response times with e-mails and voice mails, as well as delivery of product. I am also able to communicate directly with the owner or the CEO of the company when I need to get things done. I can even show up at their door without an appointment to check on my project. You simply can't do that with a big company supplier.[10]

One advantage that Locke points out very specifically is that smaller companies are often non-union shops, may be female-owned, or a minority-owned company, and that helps him achieve corporate goals. He goes on to say, "One of the things that a small supplier should ask a buyer about is their corporate goals. Find out if they have corporate goals for sourcing to women-owned or minority businesses. When I was at Chrysler, I would say yes, let's talk. When I was at American Axle, I would say yes, let's talk. At my current company, somehow we achieve those goals, but it is not part of my yearly goals as a buyer."[11]

The disadvantages of working with a small supplier have been previously mentioned, but here are a few additional points. Small suppliers are more likely to close their doors because of cash flow issues. They may not have global representation. The loss of one big client can have a significant impact on a small business. It is often the case that small suppliers become very dependent on a few big customers and literally stop their sales efforts.

Do small businesses get special treatment?

I asked both Carl Oberland and Chris Locke if smaller suppliers get a break because they are small. Or, are the expectations the same no matter what the size of the company? The answers depend on the situation. Oberland says:

> We do have a supplier qualification process for which we drop some of the criteria when, let's say, the spending is going to be less than $50,000. We may be willing to register the supplier and do less of the standard criteria than we normally do. But there is still criteria that has to be met and paperwork that gets exchanged.[12]

According to Chris Locke, his company wants all suppliers to have the same certifications. He says, "A small company can get ISO certifications just like a large company can, but we understand that a small company may have certain things that they simply can't do, specifically in the financial area, because they are small."[13] So the bottom line is that you should be prepared to compete, no matter what the size of your business.

Trends in buying: consolidating the supply base

Despite the size of the company, there are a number of buying trends that all businesses should note. Locke says, "The first is the continued movement to reduce or consolidate a company's supply base. That just makes sense. Why would you buy widgets from 10 suppliers when you can buy from two and reduce the amount of paperwork and effort, not to mention reduced costs based on higher volumes?"[14]

On the subject of consolidating suppliers, Carl Oberland takes a slightly different approach. He says that his company has made an effort to reduce the number of suppliers, but they are also looking to develop a strong stable of small businesses upon which they can rely:

We actually continue to add some players year by year in that space. The landscape differs depending upon our customer's requirements. A number of our commercial (non–public sector) customers would like us to comply with their diversity initiative within what we buy for their account. The commercial landscape is not focused on whether it is small business or big business; they tend to have stronger focus on the minority status. The federal government focuses on size of business, and then also on women-owned business, veteran-owned, hub zone area, etc. We're really starting to make a broader push or initiative across the company this year to better educate our organizations about these categories and what we are trying to do to bring more small businesses into the playing field. This is part of our own corporate responsibility philosophy, as well as a response to the corporate responsibility initiatives of our customers. Our challenge is finding the small business in a relatively efficient manner because our procurement people don't have a lot of time to spend searching.[15]

Trends in buying: cost savings

A second trend is cost savings. Here, Locke is careful to point out a few facts, "It is not about beating a supplier up to get another dime out of them. It's about working smarter. It's about the buyer asking the supplier, 'What can we do to save money? What specifications are we asking you to adhere to that are costing us money needlessly?'"[16]

Carl Oberland echoes this idea and expands upon the role of the supplier:

We call it early supplier involvement. It is an attempt to bring supplier innovation and know-how into the process very early on in the design phase, whether you are talking about products or about marketing communications. However, this early involvement is used more in areas that are not considered a commodity. For example, you don't need early supplier involvement in buying pencils. But you would employ this concept if you were designing a new type of wind turbine or a new marketing campaign. Otherwise, some of your ideas might be taking you down a path that's not really advantageous. So we try to involve that concept of early supplier involvement whenever we can.[17]

Trends in buying: faster delivery

Another trend that I have personally experienced is the need to do things faster. Projects that used to take six weeks to complete are now due in two to three weeks. The delivery of products also has a compressed time frame. Locke says, "Consumers of our products are demanding. They no longer want the same product for the next 10 years; they want a new, improved product and they want it now. We have to be able to respond to that, and we need our suppliers to respond as well."[18]

Trends in buying: global cooperation

An important trend to note is the closer cooperation amongst buyers' global counterparts. Today, buyers share information with the buyer sitting next to them and with those around the world. Locke says:

> I communicate with my counterparts in Germany and China. We're sharing information about the projects we are working on, the products we need to buy, and who we may want to buy from. Then we go to the supplier and tell them that we're interested in having them quote 1,000 widgets for me, 2,000 for the buyer in Germany, and 5,000 for the buyer in Japan. We tell them that it's critical that they bundle the widgets to provide cost savings to each of us. We are also looking further out. We might have five projects in five different countries with five different buyers. We need to know, what kind of cost saving each buyer can realize if the supplier gets all five of the projects?[19]

Trends in buying: total cost of ownership

A final trend is total cost of ownership. While this is not a new trend, it is one that is gaining momentum. When times are good, big companies just spend with very little thought. When times are bad, they look at total cost of ownership. According to Locke, that means:

> The best product, at the best value, that best fits the need. You should notice that I did not say the lowest price. I said the *best value*, and that is where total cost of ownership comes into play. If I am comparing two machines and one costs $1000 and the other costs $1,500, which one am I going to buy? I am probably going to buy the one that is $500 cheaper. But in total cost of ownership, I am looking at the cost for the 'life' of the project. So if the project is going to last two years and the cheaper machine will only last for a year, then I will have to go out and buy another one. But if the $1,500 machine is going to last two years, then it provides a lower total cost of ownership. By spending the extra $500 upfront, I'll actually save money.[20]

TIPS TO GET YOU
THINKING BIG

- Suppliers, big or small, are evaluated on the quality of their product or service, ability to deliver, and the value they provide, not just the price they bring to the customer.

- There are advantages and disadvantages for both the big and small supplier.

- Ask about corporate goals for small, female-owned, and minority-owned suppliers.

- Many large companies may have aggressive payment terms, so be prepared for how that might affect your cash flow. Some companies do offer a supplier financing program.

- Today, buyers share information with their global counterparts, so you may need to be able to provide goods and services around the world.

13

THE RFP: WHAT IT TAKES TO COMPETE

The RFP, or Request For Proposal, also known as the RFQ or Request For Quote, is enough to send small business owners running for more familiar selling situations. I almost did not respond to the first RFP I received because it seemed like a massive amount of work, and the level of detail requested was unbelievable. I did not understand some of the terminology or acronyms. Big businesses love to use terms that you can't even Google because some of them are specific to that individual company. In addition, it seemed like I would have to guess or make projections about things that I would not be able to control. Finally, all the legal language about "failure to deliver" made my eyes cross. Quite honestly, I thought it was scary. And some buyers agree.

Christopher Locke comments:

I say this tongue-in-cheek, but if I was a supplier these days with some of the Request For Quote packages that I've sent out, I would refuse it because we are asking for way too much. There is no way the supplier can read through all the specifications and respond with a price within the normal, requested time frame. Many smaller suppliers don't even read the documents, they just sign them.[1]

So what do you do when you get one of those complicated RFPs or RFQs? Ask many questions, and spend lots of time putting together your response. I got over my fear, I did the best I could, and we got the job. Twenty-five years later, we are still doing business with that big business.

There are a couple of things to note when you start to respond to requests for quotes. First, let's look at the buyers. Individuals who create RFPs for big businesses may or may not be experts in purchasing those types of goods or services. Perhaps the purchaser is really good at buying raw materials, but just does not understand how to buy training services. Very large companies do have buyers with what they call "category experience." This means that, in addition to a college education, whether it is in finance, engineering, or business, the buyer has a deep understanding of how a particular industry works. Maybe they know material handling, or plastics, or glass. Or the buyer may have acquired the expertise to buy a particular product or service over time.

Many companies have boiler plate language inserted into every RFP, even if it does not have anything to do with what is being requested. It can be confusing, and you have to wade through all of it or you might miss something. Through the years, I have learned a lot about how to respond.

For example, don't wait too long before sitting down with the often massive document to read it. If you do, you may not have enough time to devote to your response. In the past few years, I have seen companies send out RFPs with very large opportunities and a very short time frame to respond to the request. I often wonder if that is part of the strategy of the business: see if the potential supplier can respond intelligently and quickly to the RFP. That may or may not be true, but sometimes it feels that way. If you start early, you will have time to gather all your questions and get them answered.

Reading and responding to the RFP or RFQ

Most Request For Proposals have a number of different types of information, some of which may be helpful in framing your response. In a typical RFP, you will find:

- Table of contents.
- Background on the company, including its Website.
- Description of the project and deliverables. You may be asked to respond to the entire project or offered the opportunity to respond in part.
- Scope of responsibilities; what will they provide you and what are you expected to do?
- Proposal development and work schedule with specific dates, when they need a response, when

the project will be awarded, when the work must begin, and when you need to deliver. There might also be milestones that you need to reach.

◻ Specification requirements for what they need.

◻ Change requests and how billing is handled.

You should also be ready to provide detailed information about your company, including:

◻ Your company's geographic reach.

◻ Your company's capabilities.

◻ Use of subcontractors or freelancers. It is really important to note why you are using these individuals, how they will interface with your team, and your past experiences with them.

◻ Financial statements or information.

◻ Description of projects you have done that are similar in nature to the project on which you are bidding.

◻ Your approach to the project, and how you will ensure a quality product and on-time delivery.

◻ Samples of your work or product.

◻ References, certifications, and, of course, pricing.

Pay special attention to the individual that is making the request. You can usually submit questions to that person to help you develop a response. Think like a student: go through and highlight every place where you have a question so you can submit all of them at one time. If you ask intelligent questions, you start to stand out from the others that are responding. Look for gaps in the proposal and make suggestions for how they can be addressed. This may impress them and help to open a dialogue with individuals who can assist you later in the process. It is a chance for you to show them how interested you are in the company and the project.

I like to map out or group the information. You can do it on a computer, but I like to draw it out on a whiteboard, or even use stickies so I can move pieces around as I get further along. Here's how I group things.

What do I know about the company?

I like to find out about a company from research I do on my own, not just from the RFP. What is their style: formal, informal, conservative, or cutting-edge? Can I find someone who works there that can give me insight? Ask around and you might find that people you know do business with them already, or they might know people who work there.

What do I know about the project?

Why are they putting this project out to bid? Is it something they cannot or do not want to do in-house? Is this a new project or product? Are they trying to find a new supplier to replace one that is not performing? Is this a high-risk project? Is this something that is highly technical and has not been done before? Will this require research and development for you, or is it right in your wheelhouse? Is the timeline reasonable? All of this helps you understand their hot buttons. You can then use that information to write a dynamic response that is extremely targeted to what is most important to them.

What do I know about potential competitors who may be bidding?

This one can be a little tricky. Here's a tip: look at the location of the company's headquarters and other major facilities. Now use the Internet to search for your competitors that are in that region. Check their Websites and see if they make reference to the company that sent out the RFP. Many times you will find your potential competitors. However, competitors are not always those who are in direct competition with you; they may be businesses in related industries, companies that are looking to expand into your area. Doing some research will help to differentiate yourself so you have the strongest positioning possible. One other thing to note: by doing research, you may find that the RFP is just an attempt to get a current supplier to be more competitive, or that the RFP is really just a formality and you probably do not have a chance of winning it. In that case, you might want to pass and use your efforts to go after business that you do have a chance of winning.

What do I want them to know about my company?

Small businesses tend to want to tell a potential customer everything there is to know about them, including boring historical data. Resist the temptation to do that. You need to provide what is essential for the RFP reviewer to know—that gets you to a face-to-face or phone interview. Start by looking at existing proposals or marketing documents that you have already written, especially those that have won business in the past. Can some of this be repurposed or targeted for this RFP? Don't reinvent yourself, look at what you have, build on it, and customize it. What are the unique capabilities that make you a good fit for this opportunity? Do not sound like every other company; find something about you and your company that has the "wow factor" and use that.

Try to give examples of specific experiences that show you have done this type of work in the past. If you don't have something that correlates exactly, show how your experience in other situations applies here. For example, a plastics manufacturer asked us for a proposal to create a communication about a proprietary process that they believed would help them win business with an automotive manufacturer. We had never done any work in plastics and I was not familiar with extrusion machines. But I did know a lot about manufacturing, and I discovered that they were involved in lean manufacturing. This model is based upon the Toyota Production System, and is all about removing waste and becoming efficient. We had worked with a number of manufacturers that were lean, and I had even read a number of books on the subject. I leveraged that experience in the proposal and we won it.

How do I establish pricing?

This one is difficult, especially if you are in a service business. If you are providing a product, you know the cost of raw materials, labor, the margin you need, and the like. The same, however, does not hold true for services. Is an hour of your time worth more or less than an hour purchased from the competition? That depends on the level of expertise but, as a starting point, I recommend you do some research to see how your initial pricing compares to other firms in your region and across the country. This is not as tough as you might think. In fact, at one time we simply called companies and introduced ourselves. We did not try to covertly get information; we were honest in saying that we wanted to do some benchmarking of our pricing. Most were very open once they looked us up on the Internet and found out that we were legitimate. Many of my big customers have told me that price is important, but they will pay more for something if the supplier can demonstrate the value of their product or service. Of course, you still have to be competitive.

Large companies often have an idea of what they believe a project or product is worth before they send out an RFP. The trick is to figure out that number and if it is realistic for you. I call it the magic number but, actually, it is more like a range. Senior buyer Chris Locke says:

> Price will always be a consideration, but what it comes down to is education. If I say I want the best price and your price is higher, you have to educate me and tell me why. You have to explain why you have the best value for what I need. In our private lives, when we go to the store to buy something, we don't always choose the cheapest item. We choose the item that appears to have the best value and fits our needs. We may pay a little more for it because of the perceived quality, or because it provides a better outcome. That is what we are looking at when we make a global purchase,

but I may not always know that your product is the best value, which is why you have to educate me. Unfortunately, very few people do that; they just say, "here is my price."[2]

Locke uses this simple example to illustrate the point. He is going out to buy pencils, and asks three companies to submit bids:

If it is my perception that every pencil is exactly the same, I would be stupid not to pick the best price. But if the supplier educates me about his pencil, that his pencil is the only one that has an eraser so I won't have to go out and buy that separately, then I realize it's not an apples to apples comparison like I thought. Most suppliers complain that it's all about the price. But if the supplier does not educate me about his product, then price is all I have to go by.[3]

If you are doing a significant amount of business with a company, they may want to put you on a master service agreement. That means you have to give them your very best pricing, and guarantee it for the length of the project or a period of time. How much you discount is a delicate decision. Discount too much and you put yourself at risk, but discount too little and you may not be competitive. It's an art. One thing to remember is that many potential big business clients are willing to pay your price if you have value added services or faster response time.

One final note on the structure of the response: do not get creative. My experience is that big companies prefer that you to respond to each section and label it clearly. It helps them compare responses without having to search for information. It also helps them to see that you have provided all of the requested information.

Using a Scope of Work

As an option, some companies use a Scope of Work (SOW) document for new or current suppliers to understand a project and generate a quote. A Scope of Work is a little different than an RFP. It contains a high-level description of the goals, some milestones, the stakeholders, costs, and approvals. Sometimes the SOW will be very detailed if the purchaser knows exactly what he or she wants. Other times, a Scope of Work is purposely vague. Here, the purchaser is looking to see if you are creative, innovative in your approach, and able to think through the project and come up with fresh ideas.

John Kowalski puts it this way:

> I look to see if the person responding to my SOW was really listening. Do they get what I am trying to achieve, and do they really want to work on this project? I am looking for something beyond the same old thing. I can get that from a big company. There are times when a small company can come up with ideas that I have not even thought about, and that's what is great about working with a smaller firm. They make my project better and I will gladly even pay more for it when they put in the time to create something truly unique.[4]

Get creative

In addition to having a complete response, you want it to stand out. This will help you get short-listed so you actually get some face-time with the potential client to make your case. In this situation, you can think creatively when crafting a response to an RFP or SOW. For example, when we responded to an RFP for a Wiley Publishing's *For Dummies* project, we wrote it in the style of these well-known, step-by-step books. I summed up the background section on my company, Cynthia Kay and Company, by saying in "dummies language," we hope you will:

1. Use the highly committed media professionals of CK & Co.

2. Put CK & Co.'s technology to work for you.

3. Have CK & Co. create concise, friendly presentations for "Dummies."

We also printed the response to the RFP and had it bound so that it was an actual book. Yes, it was more expensive, but it was worth it. We got a contract and have been working with them since 2009.

In other cases, we have produced videos for companies to accompany their response to RFPs. If you go this route, it is a chance to put your people front and center. Let them tell the potential client how they will serve them, how they insure quality, and why they believe they can do the best job. It does not have to be highly produced, but the quality does need to be very good, and the people must be believable. You can also ask current customers to provide testimonials.

If video isn't your thing, maybe you can create an add-on print piece. Take photos of your employees or customers and use short, powerful comments that endorse your company or show why employees are excited about the project. Make it visually appealing.

Other techniques might include sending clutter busters. These are objects or samples that stand out from the typical ones, anything that will get attention and get you noticed. The cleverer you are, the better, but be careful that you do not go too far or it might backfire.

If you do the hard work of putting an RFP together and don't make the cut, don't despair. You will be able to use some of the parts and pieces for the next attempt. You should also see if the buyer will give you some constructive feedback about why you did not get the job. Some buyers will not return your request for information. But I have had great conversations after the fact with buyers who have helped me shape future RFPs.

You got short-listed. Now what?

If you get the chance to meet in person, don't waste the opportunity. As Chris Locke says:

> This is your chance to get your foot in the door and do business. This is the most important meeting of your life as far as my company is concerned. Unfortunately, most potential suppliers come in with a generic presentation, the same one they use on every company and on every department within that company. I am not just any company. I am not just

any department. I am a buyer and I have different wants, needs, responsibilities, and goals than other companies and other departments. Sell to me based on who I am, because so much of what is presented is not anything I want or need to hear. That is a waste of my time. Then, when I ask a question like, 'What are your preferred terms and conditions?' they can't give me an answer. Good luck getting another meeting with me.[5]

RFPs for government contracts

I have done a little business with our local city and county governments, but not with the federal government. However, I was recently at a White House briefing where I learned of an initiative to make it easier for small business to find out about government contracts and how to respond to RFPs. The work was spearheaded by a team of Presidential Innovation Fellows. The Website, *https://rfpez.sba.gov*, is in the start-up phase, but is supposed to help businesses create an online profile and then start bidding in "less than 10 minutes," according to the SBA. If you are interested in government business, you might want to examine and research this initiative.

TIPS TO GET YOU THINKING BIG

- Figure out how to connect with likely targets and get on a list for RFPs or SOWs.

- Spend time reading RFPs carefully. There is a lot of critical information that can be buried amongst all the legalese.

- Break the needed information into sections and tackle them one at a time.

- Use whiteboards or stickies to group information and move it around easily.

- Be sure that the information you present is customized to the opportunity. Don't use a generic approach.

- You may only get one chance at a face-to-face meeting. Be prepared to answer all the questions.

14

POSITION YOURSELF: LEARN TO BRAG

So often we are raised to be humble, not to brag about accomplishments, not to go for the awards. But recognition is important if you want to be known as an expert in your field. And who doesn't want that? After all, no one, especially big businesses, wants to work with someone who is just average.

Heidi Hennink-Kaminski, PhD, is an associate professor and Associate Dean of Graduate Studies at the University of North Carolina at Chapel Hill's School of Journalism and Mass Communication. Speaking of bragging, that's an impressive title, and she deserves it because she is an expert in her field. She is also a former small business owner and worked for a period of time for a global manufacturer.

She agrees that you need to do a little boasting, but do it responsibly:

> Bragging is fundamentally tied to the notion of setting expectations and establishing your personal 'brand promise.' Expectations need to be set intentionally and strategically. You definitely don't want to over-promise and under-deliver to clients and prospective clients. You won't stay in business for long that way. Nor do you want to under-promise and over-deliver. Although it can seem smart to always give people more than they expect, hopefully leading to positive word of mouth and endorsement, you also run the risk of not impressing some clients enough to land their business if you don't get the bragging recipe right. Another way to think about it is to carefully calibrate your bragging. So strategically, that's something that businesses really need to think about.[1]

What Heidi is talking about goes right to the very heart of your ability to attract big business—positioning. You simply must differentiate yourself from the competition. Unless this is one of your core business competencies, you might need some help here. Hennink-Kaminski says:

> I do believe that getting an outside look on your business can be money well spent. You don't necessarily need to hire somebody to do this full-time, but bringing in a consultant can be a very meaningful exercise that can pay dividends. Small, and big, businesses alike need to have an outside-in perspective

on what they offer and how they differ from competitors. Because small businesses often don't have the research or marketing budgets that large businesses do, consider tapping the freelance talent that exists today. These folks have a wealth of first-hand experience building and managing some of the most successful brands, but now work solo as consultants or within a smaller marketing services firm. Try to avoid the big firms. They need to cover their overhead, so their pricing structure is very different.[2]

I learned early on that awards are one way to differentiate your business. But an award is not an award, is not an award. Hennink-Kaminski agrees:

I'm a big fan of awards that demonstrate achieving business objectives, not necessarily vanity awards. The awards you want are the ones that demonstrate that your client got a return on their investment in you. These awards can be critical for your positioning, even if people don't know what the award stands for or what it does. When you have other organizations that are bestowing an award upon you, you have status and people pay attention.[3]

Apply for impressive awards

Some awards or activities are much more impressive than others. Before you start jumping through hoops to apply or fill out endless applications, take some time and look at the award program.

How well is it promoted? Who is sponsoring it? Are the criteria for winning clearly defined and understandable? Are the judges noteworthy? Are the judges associated with the organization that is sponsoring the award, or are they independent experts? Look to see who the past winners were. If they are well-known and respected companies, then you might want to apply.

To get started, you need to know what you are trying to accomplish and do your research. Let's say you just want greater awareness in your own community. You don't need to go for big name recognition. You do need something that will get you on the front page of the local publication or Web news. Perhaps you can apply for "Business of the Year," or "One of the 50 Most Influential Women," or "One of the 100 Best and Brightest Companies" in your region. These are awards that get local and regional press, especially if the award has a media sponsor like a local TV station or print publication.

Some of the awards you should consider are industry awards. These show that, when compared to your peers, the work is noteworthy. These awards are usually sponsored by an industry group or professional organization, and they tend to be presented annually. Even if you apply and don't win, keep trying. Read about the winners and find out what they did to stand out. If you do win, apply again. When you are consistently recognized, it shows that you have staying power. That is important to big businesses which want a stable supply base, not a business that gets lots of press one year and then falls off the map the next year.

When you fill out an award application, take the time to think about what to highlight. Don't be boring or typical and simply list how many years you have been in business, your products, etc. Instead, think about what others will consider impressive. Did you develop something that is trend-setting? Have you managed to grow your business during tough economic times? Are you teaching your peers or educating your community?

You get the idea; be creative and tell a story. It takes a lot of time and attention to apply for these awards. If you aren't going to do the hard work that it takes to win, don't bother. We spend as much time writing the application as we would on a client proposal.

Be a joiner

Another way to position yourself is to join the board of a local high-profile, non-profit organization. However, be sure that this is an organization that you really care about as people can easily spot a fake. Maybe you provide goods or services to some community effort and are recognized as a lead sponsor. Through the years, I have served on numerous boards of both non-profit and professional organizations. Rising up through the ranks of a board to serve an organization can be a big plus. For example, I joined the board of a statewide affiliate of the American Marketing Association and became president immediately. This was unusual, but the organization was in trouble. Membership was lagging, no one wanted to serve on the board, and the chapter was going to close. So why did I decide to jump in? Simple, I knew that I could turn the organization around. And if I did, that success would get me noticed by marketing professionals who I wanted to target as potential customers. After two years as the board chair, the organization was on solid ground. We had people lined up to serve, membership was growing, and the organization was financially stable.

I used that success and the contacts to make inroads for my company into the businesses of members, many of which were big local and regional businesses. Then, I did speeches around the country to other chapters about how to revitalize organizations. I got quoted in business publications and gained access to even more big businesses around the country.

That experience led me to another organization, the Small Business Association of Michigan. Once again, I was asked to be on the board and, after a few years, became the chair of the board. During my time, the organization grew from 5000 members to over 12,000, and we had numerous successful initiatives thanks to the efforts of so many. My tenure there provided the opportunity to join the National Small Business Association.

Sure, it's lots of work, but it is also a great way to show what you can do and be recognized as a leader. Once you get the recognition, you should capitalize on it. There are traditional methods to get you noticed, the usual press releases or listings that show change-ups or awards. However, I think the social media outlets have been our best sources for bragging. We routinely post pictures on Facebook of events where we are honored, and we Tweet or reTweet the news. Using LinkedIn is also a great way to spread your good news.

Social media has a number of advantages, but also requires some up-front work. Hennink-Kaminski says:

> While you can still use news releases, the days of issuing one and having it catch fire are gone. Social media and online communities can help you get known. But even in the social media space, spreading the news is not just going to happen naturally. Today, it's about deciding what you want to be known for, and then figuring out who to follow and how to get people following you. This is all about how you position yourself: What area of expertise do you want to be known for? How are you unique, or what do you provide of value? Once you've established your social network, you're ready to go. This is absolutely tied to your positioning and your brand. Start blogging, start Tweeting, start getting out there in terms of aggregating content that's related to the area for which you want to be known as an expert. Then, when you do win the award or get noticed for your work, you're going to have people who organically promote that news on your behalf.[3]

There are also some simple ways to pass along the news and brag. Add an announcement to your company phone greeting. Put a tag line on the bottom of your e-mail, or print communications, saying "the winner of..." Add press coverage to your Website. Individuals may miss initial coverage in print communications, but it lives on when it is posted on your Website.

There are many ways to brag and many reasons why you should. One thing to note, though, is be timely in the announcement of good news. Don't wait; if you do, it will quickly become old news. Also, know when to remove references. If you won Business of the Year in 2005, and your voice mail still says "Winner of Business of the Year" on your company greeting years later, you lose credibility.

Knowing how to go after recognition and then leveraging it can have a long-term impact. It adds credibility as you expand your reach and search for big customers. And, if you are looking to position your business for an acquisition, merger, or sale, the goodwill that you receive from recognition makes your firm more desirable and saleable.

TIPS TO GET YOU THINKING BIG

- Spend some time and effort to position your company in unique ways.
- Get some outside eyes to help you. Don't go for the big firms; rather, look for talented smaller companies or individuals.
- Carefully choose which awards you apply for, making sure they are not vanity awards, but awards that make good business sense.
- When you win, brag using traditional and non-traditional social media outlets.

❑ Using your skills and the resources of your company for the good of non-profit organizations can provide visibility, but don't do it unless you really care about the organization.

15

HOW TO GET FACE-TIME AND WHEN TO SHOW UP

Just try to get a meeting with a customer or potential customer. In today's hurry-up, get-it-done, and compressed days, it is next to impossible to get face-time. You send e-mails requesting a meeting, you use snail mail, and you call. The truth is that, until the business has a need or you can create a need, it's difficult, but not impossible, to get in the door. You need to pay very close attention to the opportunities or you might show up when you don't need to be there, or miss a chance to make an important connection.

One of the reasons that big businesses don't like to meet face-to-face is that they think you will use up their time talking about why they should do business with you. Most of the time, they are right. Let's face it; you want to sell to them.

That's why you may need to change the tone and content of your request for face-time.

Our company was doing business with a large firm, but we wanted to do more. Most of my attempts to gain access to the individuals who make buying decisions were largely unsuccessful, so I decided to take a different approach. I looked back over the work we had done, and made observations about how we could improve the process and reduce their costs. I talked to a number of individuals and started lobbying for an opportunity to do a short, informational seminar, not a commercial, that would help the product managers and marketers at the company develop and deliver better communications.

At first, I was told that they simply did not let suppliers have that kind of access. But I kept trying, and even sent a worksheet showing how a recent project that I worked on could have been handled more cost-effectively. It became clear that I really did have information that would help this business. I got an invitation to speak and flew across the country, at my own expense, to make the presentation. It was two days of traveling, less than 24 hours on the ground, and the face-time was just an hour and a half. Some people thought I was crazy or I didn't have enough to do. But it's not about how much time you get; it's about how you use it and what you do to make a lasting impression.

Too often, business owners get stuck doing the same old presentation without really thinking about customizing it, or adding the "wow" factor that is needed to secure business. It's like they are on auto-pilot. In this case, I prepared a full presentation that was created just for them. I always start with something that is going to surprise them, make them laugh, or get them thinking. You need to grab their attention right away, or you lose them.

I started the presentation by using dramatic examples of how communication missteps had cost companies significant dollars, loss of reputation, and the trust of their customers. The rest of the presentation was designed to help them better understand the topic, the best practices of other large companies, what they needed to do to put a good process in place, and how they could benefit. It was not about my company or our capabilities; it was about their needs. The results were even beyond what I expected. The amount of work they sent our way went up significantly and continues to this day. That is a dramatic example.

There are simpler things, however, that you can do to get face-time. I have done significant research to find a potential contact at a company, and I reached out with a very simple request: Can I have 15 minutes of your time to do "x"? You need to have a hook to get the meeting. Are you going to show them an interesting new technique, a case study that shows how implementing something new can reduce downtime, a demo of something that can improve their productivity? You get the idea. What you are offering is information, a product, or process that is geared toward helping the business solve a problem.

I have also sent out print communications with a call to action. Believe it or not, these actually received more attention than e-mails because everyone's box is stuffed with spam. In addition, many companies have stopped sending good old-fashioned print mail, so you have less competition for space on the desk of a prospect.

On one occasion, I used a series of six fun and creative postcards highlighting our services. These were highly designed and sent out every other week to large businesses we targeted. It was a mini-campaign to get us noticed, and it worked. This kind of communication can be very effective with companies that are open to using new suppliers, but don't want to let you in their door.

Some smaller businesses I know have used social media very effectively. However, I believe that bigger businesses are not as apt to pay attention to it, unless they have a very active social media presence as well. They are more likely to rely on other big businesses or partners to find good resources.

On the subject of face-time, one of the things you need to assess is the accuracy of information from your contact. On more than one occasion, I have had good initial conversations with a potential client, but was told there was no need to show up to continue the conversation or discuss materials I delivered. That's when it's time to really listen and make a judgment about the opportunity. Remember, I said if you are not sensitive to what is happening with the potential client, you might waste your time showing up or miss an important meeting.

Time to show up

Does the company have an immediate need, a new product, or a new service? Did they just restructure, or merge with another company? Are they dissatisfied with a current supplier?

Are they moving into a new area, and need the kind of expertise or products you provide? When big changes are happening at big companies, I try to press for a face-to-face meeting, even if it is a brief one. I have driven hundreds of miles, and across town; I have flown to both coasts for just a short meet-and-greet.

One potential client said very directly, "I know what you are doing and, really, you don't need to show up. We can just chat over the phone." I showed up anyway, and what I learned by sitting in the room with them was invaluable. It gave me an understanding of the company and showed me areas where we could provide service. I found out why they were walking away from a current supplier. I got a clearer picture of the pressure they were feeling from the higher-ups regarding the need to improve their products. That alone was worth the trip. We won the contract.

When you do show up, you have the chance to deepen the relationship and gain incremental business. I was working on the East Coast for a food company. I took the time to walk down the hall and visit a former client who had changed jobs and was now working for the parent company. All I intended to do was say a quick hello—that changed. I walked into the middle of a crisis she was having with a project. I spent the rest of the afternoon working with her and picked up a new project and a new client. Was it just luck that I was in the right place at the right time? Perhaps. But if I had not made the effort to connect, I would not have the new client. Think about this the next time you hesitate to show up. What might you be missing?

The time when you absolutely, positively, do need to show up is when there is a crisis or an issue that would be difficult or inappropriate to handle over the phone. When we have a crisis, I am proactive. I don't wait for the client to figure it out; I call them. If we have made a mistake, I tell them—and I tell them how we are going to fix it. If they made the mistake, I still tell them how we're going to fix it. Most companies know that, sooner or later, something will go wrong with a project or a product. "I want to know what went wrong. I don't want to blame someone, but I do want to know how are they going to fix it and what can we learn from this so it does not happen again. And, I want my supplier to be proactive, not just wait for me to call and tell them there is a problem," says John Kowalski.[1]

When things go wrong, I am amazed at how many business owners handle it by disappearing. I do just the opposite: I barrel in, make no judgments about who was right or wrong, and try to get a plan in place. You can always sort things out later, but showing up to help solve a problem gets you a lot more face-time in the future.

One more thing to consider if you are going to show up is *who* should be there. If it is a high-level meeting with executives from the C-suite, don't make the mistake of sending in someone that is not the decision-maker. Don't blow an opportunity to connect at a high level with key contacts. One business owner told me that he did not show up for just such a meeting because it was "only a half hour"—big mistake. Don't confuse the duration of a meeting with its importance; some deals happen very quickly. On the flip side, sometimes you should let others in your organization take the lead. In the case of my company, if the contact is with a highly technical expert, I like to send in my own technical experts. The discussion will be much richer and the connection deeper.

Using technology to show up

Finally, let's talk about when you should consider other ways to communicate besides face to face. For some customers, face-time is totally unnecessary. Several of my customers categorically say, "Face-time is not important to me. And I don't want to pay the travel costs associated with having someone on site." This is often the case when you work with big customers who have multiple sites. One customer told me that they value my time as much as they value their own time. It is just as easy to do a phone conference and more efficient. I have successfully used tools like Skype and GoToMeeting, but if you are going to use these methods, you need to understand a few things.

It is easy to do a bad job of presenting with these tools because it feels so casual. After all, you are sitting in your own office or location, so it might be just a little too comfortable. You need to create a great professional presence. Find a good background, not the messy part of your office or some dark corner. You can use a nice clean wall, perhaps one that has your company logo on it. Make sure the space does not have many people walking through it or noisy machines, as this will distract you and the others in on the conference. Remember to look at the camera, not down at your screen when you are talking. This establishes good eye contact even though you are miles away. Have both a really strong start and finish prepared. Finally, if possible, send materials in advance so that everyone is prepared. If you do it right, they will feel your energy and you will have saved yourself a trip. If you do it poorly, you will not make a lasting impression, and chances are you won't get any face-to-face meetings.

If your face-time is just an audio conference, you really have to ramp up your skills. You don't have the benefit of facial cues, and sometimes it is hard to interpret the tone of the conversation. That's because some people are simply not very expressive with their voice. Start by asking who is in on the call, and introduce others who might be with you. In these types of conversations, you need to listen actively and then use the technique of summarizing what you heard in order to be sure you have it right.

In today's high-tech world, you need to make the most of all methods of communication. Just being good at what you do, or having the best product or service, is not enough. How you communicate and how much you care about the relationship with your customer makes the critical difference. One customer told me, "It's obvious when I am just someone to bill, as opposed to a human being."

TIPS TO GET YOU THINKING BIG

- Understand when to show up and when to stay home.
- When things go wrong, don't hide. Show up and be proactive.
- It's not about how much time you spend; it is about the quality of the interaction.

❏ Provide content; don't just sell.

❏ Customize the information you present.

❏ When appropriate, use technology to substitute for face-to-face communication.

16

GIVE SOMETHING AWAY, GET MORE BUSINESS

Everyone likes to get something for free. Just look around and you'll see businesses that are always running some type of promotion: buy one, get one free; free samples of a product; a free trial membership; a discount through sites like Groupon or Living Social; a free iPad when you buy a flat screen TV; free software or free information. The practice of giving away something for free has escalated to the point where people expect these freebies without ever thinking about the fact that someone had to design, make, build, and market it.

So, should you consider giving something away as a sound business strategy? It's hard to think about giving away your products or services, but it can actually get you more business and entice customers who might never think about doing business with you to try you out. The first thing you need to decide is what to give away, the second is who to give it to, and the third is when to give something away. Let's examine each of these.

What to give away

I have seen businesses do giveaway programs that have nothing to do with their business. For example, a furniture store may give away the latest high-tech toy such as a free Blu-ray DVD player, or free passes to the movies, and the like. What's the problem with these types of giveaways? People take advantage of them, get the free stuff, and move on. I believe a giveaway has to be something that is at the very core of your business. This will vary dramatically from business to business. Whatever you give away, it has to be of value to the target, or you are wasting your time and money. Can you provide a potential customer with one of your products to try for 30 days? If you are in a service business, perhaps you can provide an initial consultation at no cost? Can you present a mini-workshop or class? Can you do an audit of a business's equipment or technology needs to suggest cost savings? Here's the important thing to remember: today, knowledge can set you apart.

In my business, it is not the equipment that sets us apart. Anyone who has enough money can out go and buy the cameras, editing equipment, and software. What sets us apart is the way that we think with customers, the creativity we bring to the project, and the ability to deliver a great product in a very short time frame. We will often sit down with a potential client and give them ideas. Some will say it's a bad idea to give away your ideas. In fact, there are companies that do charge for their time if they are going to provide what we refer to as creative—that is, concepts or ideas that will be implemented during a project.

When I offer to sit down and think with a potential client, I often get asked, "What will that cost me?" When I tell them that it won't cost them anything, they open their doors. That gives me the chance to show them our interest in their company, the way we work, and a sample or preview of what we can do. It also helps me shape a better response to their project or problem because I have more information. The truth is that it is harder to say no to someone who has taken the time to give you something, especially if that something is knowledge.

One of my customers asked if I would be willing to do a workshop for their communications employees at a reduced rate. They wanted me to teach them how to go out and create their own videos. The reaction of my staff was incredulous when I told them we were going to train a roomful of people to concept and shoot their own videos. Wasn't that taking business away from us? Why would we want to share the secrets and expertise that we had amassed over so many years? Would they even need us anymore? All those were really good questions. Some might say we were working our way out of a job—I thought just the opposite.

One of my staff and I presented the workshop and the results were amazing. Yes, the attendees did learn a lot about how to be do-it-yourselfers, and they went out and started to shoot more of their own video. But something else happened. They started to realize that, while they could do some of the production on their own, they still needed us for the really important or complicated projects. In fact, less than a week after the training session, my phone started to ring with requests for us to work on new projects. A number of them were projects that we would handle from start to finish. Others were projects where they would do some of the work, and we would handle the more complex tasks. What is the bottom line here? Our overall business with this customer has increased because of what we gave them.

Even if you have a tangible product, you still have knowledge to give away. Can you help your customer or potential customer use the product more effectively or help them reduce their costs? Can you share some of your best practices? Whatever you can give away in terms of knowledge gets your customer more engaged with you and generally results in more business.

Who is a great target for a giveaway?

Once you've decided what to give away, you want to develop a clear picture of who to target. Obviously, the people who have expressed an interest in your product or service are a no-brainer. But you need to look at whether or not there is potential there for long-term business. We have a profile that we have developed over the years of what our ideal customer looks like. In our case, it is a company that is forward-thinking, has ongoing needs that will bring us business at least several times a year (preferably more), and who want a long-term relationship. So when we do a giveaway, we look first to see if the company matches our ideal customer profile. We also look at doing giveaways for our existing customers which might encourage them to buy products and services that they are not currently using.

When do you give something away?

The most common time to do a giveaway is when you are trying to get the potential big customer in your door. But giveaways are also appreciated when your customer is facing difficult times. Many of our large customers have faced significant challenges during the economic downturn; they have closed facilities and reduced their workforce. They simply don't have the resources that were once available. In one case, we got a heads-up that our client was in dire straits and was preparing to slash budgets. We decided to be proactive and asked for a meeting. We offered to help them figure out the best way to use the budget they did have, even though it was significantly less than the previous year. By leveraging some existing assets and discounting our time, we were able to provide a plan that would help them continue to market their products. We were essentially giving away some of our time. Is that smart? Should we have held out for a customer that was able to pay full price for our services? It's a judgment call because once you discount, you may not be able to get back to charging full price.

In this case, however, the strategy worked. We helped our customer through a difficult time. As business improved and budgets got bigger, we got the business back. It can be risky to give away too much, but it can also cement and grow a relationship. It's amazing what kind of reaction you get when you give away something to big customers who are used to paying for everything as a line item. Best of all, you not only get their business, you may also get recommended to their circle of suppliers and colleagues.

A word of caution

Mark Peters agrees with me to a point. But he adds some words of caution about giving away too much:

> You have to understand the opportunity with a big company, and you have to manage your own risks. There are all kinds of risks in doing free quoting, and giving up your intellectual property in the hopes of getting some business, which may never come through. And that kind of thing happens to small companies with big companies all the time. But if you know how to manage the risks early on in the negotiation, get them interested in what you do and what you can do for them, it's a great relationship. I also believe that a supplier should get paid for true research and development, because product development cycles can be quite long and the product may never be produced.[1]

Giving back

Finally, there is another type of giveaway: giving back to the community. This is another way to attract big business. For many large companies, making the world a better place is a part of their mission, their corporate DNA. These companies often have formal programs and volunteer opportunities for their employees. They also seek out and notice small companies that share their values with respect to supporting non-profit organizations with time, money, or *pro bono* services.

We routinely give away media production services to non-profit organizations in our area. Sometimes, these are the same organizations that our big customers are supporting. That's great because it gives us the chance to connect on a different level. Beware, however, that you don't invest in your community just to get noticed. And don't expect that it will come back to you, as often it does not. If you do this simply as a way to strengthen current relationships, you may be disappointed. And, yes, some people do take advantage of your kind and generous spirit.

For example, a local organization, which is affiliated with a worldwide organization, needed help to get started in our community. We donated a number of video productions, at a significant dollar value, to help them raise money for a building and to promote awareness of their cancer programs. As the years went by, we continued to help and provided services at a reduced rate. One day, the executive director called to say that they would not be using our services for their annual luncheon. One of their board members was going to fund the project, but insisted on using another media production company. Here was the real zinger: she asked if we would allow the other company to use video that we had acquired over the years. To her credit, she felt terrible. I did too, but decided that the work of the organization was more important to me than anything else. I reminded myself that we were giving something away because we believe that giving back is as important to our business as it is to the organization that benefits. It helps you think outside of yourself. It provides an outlet for people's talents and, without getting too sappy, it just feels good.

TIPS TO GET YOU
THINKING BIG

- Find creative ways to give potential and current customers something of value.

- When you give something for free, or through discount, be sure that you have assessed the potential opportunities—otherwise you might be wasting the effort.

- Understand the risks of sharing your intellectual property.

- Giving back to the community is a great way to connect on a whole different level with new audiences, but don't do it unless you really believe in the effort.

17

Find a Champion and Perform

I learned early on that, to get anything done, someone has to own it. This is especially true in big businesses. When a big business wants to launch a new product, support a cause, change processes and procedures, or transform the culture, someone has to be the champion. That person, or group of people, is focused on getting the job done, and making sure the effort is successful. If the effort or initiative is a large, high-profile one, the champion is often a member of the executive leadership team. And, if it is a really big deal, it is the CEO, or even the chairman of the board.

If you are a small business that is looking to work with big business, you also need to find a champion or two. So what exactly is a champion, and how can they help you? I'll give you a hint: it's not always who you think it is.

To begin with, the person who might be your champion at a big business is probably not the CEO, or even a vice president. These folks are generally hard to get to because they are often being pulled in so many directions. What you are looking for is someone who has the ability to exert the influence necessary to get you in the door and coach you through the process of establishing a relationship that turns into big business. Who is that person? It's the person who has a need, is experiencing some pain, is trying to chart a new course, or is just someone who really loves your product or service. If you are responding to an RFP, the champion might very well be the person buying the product or service. Of course, they don't know that they are going to be your champion. At least not yet! You'll have to win them over.

A number of years ago, we responded to a Request For Proposal. There was a contact name for questions. After thoroughly reading the RFP, I developed a series of questions about what was needed, including a few questions that pointed out some significant gaps that might cause issues in the delivery of the product. I e-mailed them and asked if we could chat. The conversation started out in a very formal tone. But as it continued, it became obvious to the buyer that what I was asking could help her streamline the project, and maybe even cut some costs. I also found out that the company had previously contracted for this type of work and was disappointed. The project was over budget, and the results just were not there. She had been burned and did not intend for that to happen again. We responded and won the contract. Then we made this buyer look really good; we delivered ahead of schedule and on budget. We had our champion. When another project surfaced, she alerted us that the

RFP was coming and had a very tight turnaround for the response. She also provided some guidance on what had been budgeted. That was valuable information which helped us frame a response that was appropriate for what they wanted to spend.

A champion is also important because, in a larger company, there are so many pockets of business that you, as an outsider, simply can't find them all. A champion will recommend you to their colleagues, give you information about what is important to the company, and perhaps get you on a preferred supplier list.

A champion or two

You should also seriously consider having a number of champions at a company because big businesses are constantly shifting people around. Therefore, it is likely that today's champion may not be in a position to help you tomorrow. You can minimize this particular risk by working to develop relationships at various levels of the company.

Mark Peters takes a slightly different approach to the idea of having more than one champion. He says:

I literally had an "ah-ha moment" years ago listening to a presentation on negotiating with big companies. When you go into a sales presentation with a big company, there is rarely any *one* person at a table who can say "yes." But if anyone at the table says "no," that one person can kill the relationship. You don't need all of them to be advocates. You need one or two of them. Try to figure out the person in your organization who matches up best with key individuals in their organization. It might be the purchasing department; it might be the quality department; it might be the distribution department. You need somebody at that table to say, "I love working with that company, and it's going to cost us a lot if we switch or don't hire them." It's different with different customers, but you need to find that key connection point. And it could be in a number of areas.[1]

Pull out all the stops

When you do make it onto that list or get that job, you have to actually outperform what is expected. Make your champion look good. That means everything from pulling out all the stops, to delivering something on a ridiculous timetable, to helping your champion when they don't have the budget for a project.

For example, we received a last minute call from a client. They had been short-listed and had an opportunity to win a massive global contract. They needed some help to put together an RFP that would really stand out. I could have just created something based on the information they had, but I really wanted to help this champion because they were taking a chance on working with us in a new and different way. I started to think about how I might get some inside information that would be valuable. I combed through my contacts, and came across someone who used to do business with my client's potential client. Then I made a call and asked if he still had contacts that might be able to help. The answer was yes, in fact, there was a recently retired executive who might provide some information. I wrote a list of questions and we received the answers. We developed a very non-traditional, creative presentation that really impressed my customer's potential customer. They won the global contract, and I got another champion who told the story of how we helped them to many others in the company.

In another case, a potential client came to us for some assistance with the rollout of a new employee discipline program. We helped them revise the plan and think through the consequences of the timetable which would have different groups of employees (within the same facility) operating under different rules. We helped them figure out a way to streamline the process. As a result, they looked like heroes to upper management. By the way, we did not take credit for the work. By making your champion look good, you deepen the relationship and generally win more business.

Finally, when looking for champions, don't discount those who don't have a title or don't seem to be big players. You might be surprised as sometimes the champion is the quiet influencer behind-the-scenes. Think about the executive assistant, the project manager, the store clerk, the receptionist—they all know things that you need to know if you want to get into a company and grow the business. Most of them are happy to share information with someone who is authentic about their intensions, respectful of their time, and truly grateful for their efforts. Go find yourself a champion or two, and watch what happens.

TIPS TO GET YOU THINKING BIG

◻ Try to identify individuals who can provide you with information and be your champion; it might be a behind-the-scenes player.

◻ If at all possible, have a number of individuals in different areas to help you make connections.

◻ Think about which individuals in your organization match up well with the champion.

◻ Pull out all the stops to make your champion look good—they got you in the door and can keep the business coming.

18

When It Comes to Operations, Think Like a Big Business

When it comes to operations, it's easy for small business owners to consider themselves minor players. Because they're small, they think they don't need the systems, procedures, and safeguards that huge companies do. Actually, it is very important for small businesses to have these systems, because there are fewer people to shoulder the work.

Have a system for everything

So where are some of the areas to think big? According to Bob Fish, it is every aspect of the business. He says, "I really do believe in systematizing everything. Take what is routine and mundane, and create a system around it. Then anybody can execute it. That frees up your mind to take care of the vision, and whatever is important to the company."[1] There are some things that are easy to systematize in the coffee business, such as how to express espresso, but Fish says others are not so obvious: "We have a system for how to greet a customer; how to have a chat with a customer at the end of the counter, and so on. The systems end up becoming the playbook for the company. A company needs that playbook or roadmap. Without it, we're just a bunch of individuals, and we might all go in different directions. But because we're tied together by a system, it's what allows us to grow so fast."[2]

At Cynthia Kay and Company, we also believe in having systems in place. In fact, we have documented, step by step, almost all of our processes and procedures. For example, there are endless types and sizes of video files. We have created profiles for each of our clients so that we know exactly what to provide them each time, no matter who is working on the project. When a specification for a customer changes, we document it. It's important to have one central location where you put all your documentation. Everything needs to be easy for everyone to find and update.

We also use time-tracking programs so we can accurately report to our clients where we are with regard to the budget. We use an electronic dashboard to track every project, including where it is in the process ("on fire" means we are on deadline), who is working on it, any special instructions, and more. By having this dashboard visible on a large plasma screen, as well as on every employee's computer, we can be sure that everyone is in sync. We also have a system for how all field equipment should be stored. That way everyone knows where it is every time, and we won't accidentally leave anything behind when we go out to a job site.

Think about quality and delivery

Of course, just because you have a system in place does not mean that you are producing a quality product or service, or that you can deliver on-time. If you want to attract and retain big customers, you have to assure them that your quality will not be an issue or put their brand at risk. According to Mark Peters:

> The biggest driver for big, especially branded companies is brand risk. We now have an international certification for our quality systems. You simply have to do the hard work to be sure that you will not put your customer's brand at risk, whether that is by not delivering, or a safety issue, or a quality standard issue. You also have to be able to 'plug and play' with their logistics systems. A lot of small companies don't get that. They come in with a product, but they don't understand how the other pieces of their business put their customer's brand at risk. And so they don't get asked to the table.[3]

Charles Phaneuf, owner of CE Rental, agrees with Peters, and offers three tricks that have helped his operation. He says:

> Quality has to be the primary operational outcome, and cost has to be close behind to continue operating. Quality brings customers back. Cost control keeps

pricing competitive and keeps us alive to be there for the returning customer. When an operation gets to a point that it produces a quality outcome at a competitive cost, the first trick is to "lock it in" to get the desired result to repeat. Then, like a big company, the entrepreneur can define a process, function, or job, and hand it off to an employee so the entrepreneur can move on to the next process or function that needs to be defined, debugged, and developed. Slowly, the entrepreneur builds structure that can carry on and function independent of the entrepreneur, much like a big company. The second trick is to remain close to the operation and continue to measure results, and evolve those processes or functions. The third trick is to get the organization to monitor and improve itself by training employees to think and act like entrepreneurs. Then the entrepreneur has something that won't be a burden to operate and is saleable, if and when the entrepreneur is ready.[4]

Gear up for electronic invoicing and payment

Another key area where you need to think big, or big companies simply won't work with you, is in the electronic handling of transactions, from purchase through the payment process. Almost every large company we work with is trying to eliminate paperwork. They don't want to have to physically open invoices that have been mailed and scan them into their system. They don't want to have to print checks. Paying electronically is an important part of the supplier registration process. You will need to invoice electronically, using your customer's portal. In all honesty, it takes a little getting used to, but most of them have a help system and supplier training to get you started. You also need to provide your customer with your bank and account routing numbers.

According to Carl Oberland:

> Small businesses have to be able to gear up and be flexible. If a small business is doing business with 10 clients, they might all have a different invoicing portal. So the small business is going to have to know how to deal with each one. If the small business has a lot of business, they can put an EDI [electronic data interchange] automatic exchange between their mainframe and the client's mainframe. But that typically is for bigger companies because it's a bigger investment in the EDI setup and data monitoring.[5]

Think lean

Many big companies spend time and money for studies showing how to eliminate waste and become more efficient. It's called "lean," and it has its roots in a system designed by Toyota. Since then, many manufacturers, healthcare organizations, and others have adopted the principles. But this strategy is not just for big organizations. I was first introduced to the concept by Herman Miller when it instituted the Herman Miller Production System, based upon the Toyota Production System. Since then, a number of my clients have moved towards being lean. I paid attention and started to think about how it could be applied on a smaller scale to Cynthia Kay and Company.

My company consistently evaluates our processes, and we make changes to be more efficient. It does not take much to figure out what you need to change. Just look at the areas of your business where you are experiencing a bottleneck or wasted time. You don't need to do a big study. You do, though, need to ask questions of your employees, and search for solutions. However, it's not always about *doing* something; sometimes it's best *not* to do anything. For example, we used to track every activity in our media production process. That was time-consuming, so we decided to prioritize the activities and only track those that had a real impact on the work. By eliminating some of the busy work of tracking non-essential tasks, we have more time to concentrate on the important aspects of our business. One thing to note: ask your big customers what is important to them. Take that information and be sure to track or provide what they need. It might seem insignificant to you, but they have very definite requirements, and you need to be aware of them.

Big businesses routinely use outside resources. This is an area where my organization thinks big too. Do we really need to be employment specialists? Do we need to be accounting and tax specialists? Do we need to be IT professionals? The answer is no. That's why we have put into place the resources that help our operation become leaner, better, and more efficient. How well you operate your business is important to your big customers. You need to be sure that things run smoothly so you don't let them down.

TIPS TO GET YOU
THINKING BIG

- Have a system for everything; it becomes the playbook for your organization.

- Document all your critical processes and procedures, and keep the information in one central location.

- Make sure that you provide a quality product or service every time. Do not put your customer's brand at risk.

- Gear up for electronic invoicing and payment, or you just won't be able to work with big customers.

- Think lean. Eliminate waste in your systems, and become efficient so you can respond quickly to big customer requests.

19

KNOW WHEN NOT TO COMPETE

It's easy to think that you should respond to every opportunity to grab business with large customers who have many needs. This is especially true for fledgling businesses. Knowing when *not* to compete might be the most important lesson for saving your business from ruin. There are a number of questions a small business can ask to help determine if they should go for it or take a pass. A few of them include:

- Does the work really fit into your core capabilities, or will it require you to learn a whole new set of skills that are too far away from your mission?

- Will it put you in a position where one big client is using up so much of your capacity that it puts you at risk for meeting commitments to other customers?

- Can you ramp up quickly enough to meet their needs?

- Will the client be so much of a hassle that you start to resent doing the work?

- Will you have to respond to so many fires that you start to confuse motion with profitability?

- Can you hit their magic number without doing major damage to your bottom line?

I learned this lesson by watching my big business clients chase after work, spend lots of money trying to win it, and then lose out or abandon the effort. The best example of this was a well-respected manufacturer of systems. This company had the opportunity to bid on a very large project, perhaps the largest one in the company's history. The effort to respond to the RFP alone was huge. Engineers were pulled off of projects and assigned to work on the response. Designs were created, costs were calculated, prototypes and animations were made, PowerPoint presentations and videos used, etc. The work consumed a tremendous amount of manpower over the course of almost a year, not to mention all the outside resources that they brought in to help, including my team.

When the big day came, my client presented and walked away feeling relieved that it was over, and was optimistic about their chances. Not long after, they were informed that they did not get the job. I was in my office working late that night when the CEO called to thank me for the work and tell me that they were not successful. I felt terrible. They spent a lot of money with us trying to win the business. But then he said something that floored me: "I am not sorry we lost. In fact, I am relieved. I have been lying awake at night trying to figure out where we would find all the qualified engineers we need to accomplish this project, not to mention the risk of devoting so many of our resources to this one customer." The good news was that they did not get the job. The bad news was they were so focused on one opportunity for the whole year, that they missed out on others which might have been better for the company. If they had chosen not to compete, they would have had the resources to go after those other projects.

Years later, I remembered that situation when we were asked to bid on a project that would have literally put us at capacity for a number of months. I had to take stock of what it would do to our ability to serve our other clients. Was it worth the risk? I decided not.

When to say no

It's hard to say no when you see the business right in front of you, but there are other things to consider. What are the consequences of piling on more work than your staff can handle? Will you be able to deliver the amount of product needed if your operation doesn't have the capacity? How long would it take you to develop that capacity, and what happens in the meantime? Is there a competitor who is more efficient than you are, and is able to produce what is needed at a lower cost? I am not suggesting that you make it all about cost. There have also been times when we have been asked to lower our price to be more competitive. We have walked away from some of those situations because we believed that our competition was not being realistic about the real cost of the project.

Most small business owners who work with big businesses generally have a process for evaluating an opportunity. They have key questions that they use to filter out the good ones, and recognize the ones that are suspect. Mark Peters says there are a few things that tip him off and send him running in the opposite direction:

> A lot of times in our business, price becomes the issue. And so, if a customer is looking for a particular product, we ask, what do you want the product to do and what do you want the price per serving to be? If we're trying to hit a price point, we need to know what the price point is. So if a customer, or a potential customer, doesn't want to share that information, we tell them that we need to have a transparent relationship, so that we can do the best job. There is a lot of fear when you work with a big company because they can take a great idea and scale it. So requesting and demanding a level of transparency—both ways—has been hugely beneficial for us and our customers. On the other hand, if the information is not available or it's sketchy, we've got other opportunities that we go ahead and act on. We're fortunate that we don't need to compete for every opportunity. There are other

companies that will gladly chase those rabbits. Let them go do it.[1]

A different way to compete

Sometimes it is not about a product or service. Instead, it is about competing for a certain market. The owners of CE Rental in Raleigh, North Carolina, decided to stop trying to compete with much larger companies in their market shortly after they purchased the company. They could not duplicate the large inventory of the bigger companies. They didn't have the trucks or the personnel to handle some jobs. They did not have the advertising or marketing budgets to get them noticed, so they decided on a different approach. They would offer very unique products to their rental customers in an effort to attract a very specific target market. They sought out interesting patterns of china and glasses, instead of the typical ones that everyone else offered. They started to sew their own linens, chair covers, and other accessories. That meant they could create unique environments for events. They would provide very personal service: sitting down multiple times with an event planner, doing a site survey, accommodating unusual pick-up and drop-off times.

It did not take long for this small company with very niche products and amazing service to get noticed. By not competing in the traditional way, and offering an alternative to the larger companies, this small company has grown into a multi-million dollar company. And here is the really interesting part of the story. The big companies have tried to buy this little company to get rid of them and the competition.

Balance the mix of big and small customers

Choosing to compete is not just about stretching to reach new goals (that's always important for a business), it's also about carefully considering the kind of business you want and don't want. And here is one final thought. While I have spent a lot of time talking about connecting with and winning big business, you need to carefully balance your mix of big and small customers.

Big customers require a big commitment and, depending upon the type of business, a significant investment in additional people or equipment. Therefore, you might not want to compete for every large customer or project that comes along. Consider balancing your customer portfolio with some mid-sized or small companies. In the end, it's all about operating the best small business possible so you can compete and win the customers who are the best fit for your small business.

TIPS TO GET YOU
THINKING BIG

- Don't think you have to compete for every opportunity.
- Carefully assess the pros and cons of competing, and how a win will impact your organization.

- Your best customers will share information with you so that you can provide the best possible price and product.

- Assess your customer mix. Competing for every big customer or job might be too much of a stress on your ability to respond.

NOTES

Chapter 1

1. "Frequently Asked Questions about Small Business." September 2012, *www.sba.gov/sites/default/files/FAQ_Sept_2012.pdf.*

2. "Is Your Small Business a Microbusiness? If So, You May Be In Luck!" March 2009, *www.sba.gov/community/blogs/community-blogs/small-business-matters/your-small-business-microbusiness-if-so-you-m.*

3. Landis, Marilyn D. Interview by author. February, 2013.

4. Kowalski, John. Interview by author. February, 2013.

5. Ibid.

6. Peters, Mark. Interview by author. January, 2013.

Chapter 2

1. Fish, Bob. Interview by author. January, 2013.

Chapter 3

1. Price, Rachael. Interview by author. March, 2013.

2. Ibid.

3. Ibid.

Chapter 4

1. Brogan, Molly. "2012 Small Business Access to Capital Survey." July 11, 2012, *www.nsba.iz/?p=3462.*

2. Ibid.

3. "2012 U.S. Small Business Banking Satisfaction Study." November 9, 2012, *www.jdpower.com/content/press-release/5wxWIuZ/2012-u-s-small-business-banking-satisfaction-study.htm.*

4. Dunlap, Jim. Interview by author. February 2013.

5. Ibid.

6. Ibid.

7. Ibid.

8. Ibid.

9. Ibid

10. Brogan, Molly. "2012 Small Business Access to Capital Survey." July 11, 2012, *www.nsba.z/?p=3462*.

11. Dunlap, Jim. Interview by author. February 2013.

12. Brogan, Molly. "2012 Small Business Access to Capital Survey." July 11, 2012, *www.nsba.z/?p=3462*.

13. Landis, Marilyn D. Interview by author. February, 2013.

14. Ondeckcapital.com, accessed June 2013, *www.ondeckcapital.com/*.

15. Landis, Marilyn D. Interview by author. February, 2013.

16. Ibid.

17. Ibid.

18. Dunlap, Jim. Interview by author. February 2013.

19. Landis, Marilyn D. Interview by author. February, 2013.

Chapter 5

1. Landis, Marilyn D. Interview by author. February, 2013.

Chapter 6

1. "Workplace Wellness Programs in Small Business: Impacting the Bottom Line." June/July, 2012, *www.nsba.biz/wp-content/uploads/2012/09/well-ness-survey-v3.pdf.*

2. Chandler, Nathan. Interview by author. March, 2013.

Chapter 7

1. Phaneuf, Vicki. Interview by author. March, 2013.

Chapter 8

1. Peters, Mark. Interview by author. January, 2013.

2. Ibid.

3. Phaneuf, Vicki. Interview by author. March, 2013.

Chapter 9

1. Fish, Bob. Interview by author. January, 2013.

Chapter 11

1. Fish, Bob. Interview by author. January, 2013.
2. Ibid.
3. Ibid.
4. Ibid.
5. Ibid.
6. Ibid.

Chapter 12

1. Oberland, Carl. Interview by author. February, 2013.
2. Ibid.
3. Peters, Mark. Interview by author. January, 2013.
4. Oberland, Carl. Interview by author. February, 2013.
5. Ibid.
6. Locke, Christopher. Interview by author. February, 2013.
7. Ibid.
8. Ibid.
9. Ibid.
10. Ibid.
11. Ibid.

12. Oberland, Carl. Interview by author. February, 2013.

13. Locke, Christopher. Interview by author. February, 2013.

14. Ibid.

15. Oberland, Carl. Interview by author. February, 2013.

16. Locke, Christopher. Interview by author. February, 2013.

17. Oberland, Carl. Interview by author. February, 2013.

18. Locke, Christopher. Interview by author. February, 2013.

19. Ibid.

20. Ibid.

Chapter 13

1. Locke, Christopher. Interview by author. February, 2013.

2. Ibid.

3. Ibid.

4. Kowalski, John. Interview by author. February, 2013.

5. Locke, Christopher. Interview by author. February, 2013.

Chapter 14

1. Hennink-Kaminski, Heidi. Interview by author. February, 2013.
2. Ibid.
3. Ibid.

Chapter 15

1. Kowalski, John. Interview by author. February, 2013.

Chapter 16

1. Peters, Mark. Interview by author. January, 2013.

Chapter 17

1. Peters, Mark. Interview by author. January, 2013.

Chapter 18

1. Fish, Bob. Interview by author. January, 2013.
2. Ibid.

3. Peters, Mark. Interview by author. January, 2013.

4. Phaneuf, Charles. Interview by author. March, 2013.

5. Oberland, Carl. Interview by author. February, 2013.

Chapter 19

1. Peters, Mark. Interview by author. January, 2013.

Index

About the Author

Cynthia Kay is a passionate spokesperson for small business—speaking, teaching, and coaching small business owners, all while running an award-winning company. For more than 25 years, Cynthia Kay and Company has produced high-quality communications that are used on the national and international scene. The company serves a variety of businesses and enterprises, from Fortune Global 100 corporations to small businesses and non-profit organizations.

A graduate of Michigan State University, Kay also holds a Master's Degree in Communications. She has been honored four times as one of the 50 Most Influential Women in West Michigan. The company has been named twice as one of West Michigan's 101 Best and Brightest Companies and has earned a number of Telly Awards. Kay serves on the Board of the National Small Business Association (NSBA). She lives in Grand Rapids, Michigan.